Knits for the Modern Baby

Vice President and Chief Operations Officer: Tom Siebenmorgen
Vice President, Sales and Marketing: Pam Stebbins
Vice President, Operations: Jim Dittrich
Editor in Chief: Susan White Sullivan
Director of Designer Relations: Debra Nettles
Senior Art Director: Rhonda Shelby
Senior Prepress Director: Mark Hawkins

Produced for Leisure Arts, Inc. by Penn Publishing Ltd.
www.penn.co.il
Editor: Shoshana Brickman
Design and layout: Ariane Rybski
Technical editing: Rita Greenfeder
Photography by: Danya Weiner

PRINTED IN CHINA

EAN/ISBN-13: 978-1-60140-872-3
ISBN-10: 1-60140-872-2
Library of Congress Control Number: 2009924835

Cover photography by Danya Weiner

Knits for the Modern Baby

21 Fresh Designs for Newborn to 24 months

by

LENA MAIKON

A LEISURE ARTS PUBLICATION

Contents

❀ Introduction ❀

There is something special about knitting for children. It means thinking about the child with every stitch you knit; it means giving an item that is filled with love, warmth, and positive thoughts. Knitting for children isn't only inspired by a desire to dress children in clothes that are cute, comfortable, and soft; making children's clothing by hand just seems so natural. Like preparing homemade applesauce, or baking a birthday cake from scratch.

All of the garments in this book were designed with children—and their parents—in mind. The items are fashionable and fun, stylish and easy to wear. There are plenty of items for keeping warm during winter, including hats with earflaps, sweaters, vests, and warm fuzzy socks. You'll also find items that are perfect for spring and early autumn, such as lightweight cardigans, roomy jumpers, and breezy overalls. All of the items are sure to become favorites; clothes that will be worn, cherished, and saved long after their original wearers have outgrown them.

Every article of clothing is cozy and sensible—nothing to make kids itch, fuss, or feel constricted. The clothes are comfortable enough to wear while playing in a park, and pretty enough to put on for a party. Parents will find that the garments are easy to put on and take off, as they are designed with a minimal amount of buttons and ties.

As for the toys and blankets, these were tried and tested by my son and his friends, and all of them received excellent grades. They were hugged, played with, tossed about, and snuggled, perfect proof that kids like them. These items were designed with a sense of old-fashioned style, and made with materials that are totally touchable.

There is something for knitters of every skill level in this book, and even the more challenging projects can be accomplished with a bit of patience and effort. As for the selection of yarns, I have tried to use blended yarns that include cotton and wool, and are soft and pleasant to the touch.

The colors are classic and gentle, a variety of hues that are soothing and sweet. In the boys' clothing, you'll find forest greens, earthy browns, and rich blues. In the girls' clothing, there are pastel pinks, royal burgundies and purples, and minty greens. There are also many items featuring yellows, greens, oranges, and whites. These are perfect for boys and girls who love a variety of colors.

About the author

Lena Maikon learned to knit from her grandmother at the age of five in her hometown of Novosibrisk, Russia . She didn't pick up her knitting needles for thirty years, but started to knit again as a form of creative therapy. This quickly turned into a passion and profession. Lena often uses unconventional materials in her designs, and dreams of creating a knitted world. She knits and crochets socks, shoes, dresses, handbags, flowers, vases, and light fixtures. She has published two creative knitting books, and has her own handmade clothing and accessory label, **Leninka**. Lena is the mother of two sons who love to wear fuzzy knitted sweaters and cozy socks. They are the sources of inspiration for many of the projects in this book.

General Instructions

Standard Yarn Weight System

Yarn Weight Symbol & Names	LACE 0	SUPER FINE 1	FINE 2	LIGHT 3	MEDIUM 4	BULKY 5	SUPER BULKY 6
Type of Yarns in Category	Fingering, size 10 crochet thread	Sock, Fingering, Baby	DK, Light Worsted	DK, Light Worsted	Worsted, Afghan, Aran	Chunky, Craft, Rug	Bulky, Roving
Knit Gauge Range* in Stockinette St to 4" (10 cm)	33-40** sts	27-32 sts	23-26 sts	31-24 sts	16-20 sts	12-15 sts	6-11 sts
Advised Needle Sized Range	000-1	1 to 3	3 to 5	5 to 7	7 to 9	9 to 11	11 and larger

*GUIDELINES ONLY: The chart above reflects the most commonly used gauges and needle sizes for specific yarn categories.

** Lace weight yarns are usually knitted on larger needles to create lacy openwork patterns. Accordingly, a gauge range is difficult to determine. Always follow the gauge stated in your pattern.

KNIT TERMINOLOGY

United States	International
gauge	tension
bind off	cast off
yarn over (YO)	yarn forward (yfwd) or yarn around needle (yrn)

CROCHET TERMINOLOGY

United States	International
slip stitch (slip st)	single crochet (sc)
single crochet (sc)	double crochet (dc)
half double crochet (hdc)	half treble crochet (htc)
double crochet (dc)	treble crochet (tr)
treble crochet (tr)	double treble crochet (dtr)
treble double crochet (dtr)	triple treble crochet (ttr)
triple treble crochet (tr tr)	quadruple treble crochet (qtr)
skip	miss

SKILL LEVELS

■□□□ Beginner	Projects for first-time knitters using basic knit and purl stitches. Minimal shaping.
■■□□ Easy	Projects using basic stitches, repetitive stitch patterns, simple color changes, and simple shaping and finishing.
■■■□ Intermediate	Projects with a variety of stitches, such as basic cables and lace, simple intarsia, doublepointed needles and knitting in the round needle techniques, mid-level shaping and finishing.
■■■■ Experienced	Projects using advanced techniques and stitches, such as short rows, fair isle, more intricate intarsia, cables, lace patterns, and numerous color changes.

KNITTING NEEDLES

U.S.	0	1	2	3	4	5	6	7	8	9	10	10½	11	13	15	17
U.K.	13	12	11	10	9	8	7	6	5	4	3	2	1	00	000	---
METRIC - MM	2	2.25	2.75	3.25	3.5	3.75	4	4.5	5	5.5	6	6.5	8	9	10	12.75

CROCHET HOOKS

U.S.	B-0	C-2	D-3	E-4	F-5	G-6	H-7	I-9	J-10	K-10½	N	P	Q
METRIC - MM	2.25	2.75	3.25	3.5	3.75	4	5	5.5	6	6.5	9	10	15

Materials and Tools

Yarn Selection

To make an exact replica of the photographed items, use the yarns listed in the Materials section of the projects. All of these yarns are readily available in the United States and Canada at time of printing.

www.coatsandclark.com

www.spinriteyarns.com

www.lionbrand.com

Buttons, paillettes, and bells

These are used to add decorative touches. Though the size is specified in each project, feel free to adjust as desired.

Elastic string

This is used to make a bell shape in the Garden of Delight Pullover.

Felt

This is used to decorate the Six-Sided Soft Toy.

Holders

These are used to hold stitches while other stitches are being worked.

Leather hole punch

This is used to punch holes in leather pieces in Booties Made for Walking.

Leather pieces

These are used to make sturdy soles on Booties Made for Walking.

Needles and hooks

Some of the projects use basic single-pointed knitting needles. Others use a set of five double-pointed needles, circular needles, or cable needles. Several projects include crocheted enhancements that are made using a single crochet hook. Many projects use more than one set of needles.

Polyester fiberfill stuffing

This is used to stuff the Six-Sided Soft Toy and Huggable Snuggable Bunny.

Remnant yarns

These are used to connect the sides of the Six-Sided Soft Toy, and to attach felt decorations.

Scissors

Use these to cut yarn, thread, and templates.

Sewing needle and thread

These are used to sew on buttons, beads, and other adornments. Be sure to use sturdy thread so that adornments are sewed on securely.

Stitch marker

This can be used to mark stitches while you work.

Tracing paper, pencil, and permanent marker

These are used to copy templates and transfer them to leather or cardboard.

Yarn needle

This is used to sew seams. Make sure the eye of the needle is wide enough to thread the yarn.

Basics

Blocking

This is an important step in finishing the knitting process, and the best way to shape pattern pieces and make knitted edges smooth before sewing the pieces together. Choose your method of blocking according to the label on your yarn. If you are in doubt, do a test block on your gauge swatch.

Charts

Charts are helpful for following colorwork and other stitch patterns at a glance. When knitting back and forth in rows, read chart from right to left on right side (RS) rows, and from left to right on wrong side (WS) rows. Repeat any stitch and row repeats as directed in the pattern. To keep track of your place, try placing a self-adhesive note on the chart under the row you are working on, and move the note after every row.

Cleaning

Check the label on your yarn to determine the best way of washing and drying your knitted item. Most of the yarns used in these projects require hand washing, or machine washing on a gentle or wool cycle using mild detergent. Do not agitate knitted items, and don't soak them for more than 10 minutes. If you are hand washing the items, rinse with lukewarm water to remove detergent. Fold wet items in a towel to press out water, then lay flat to dry in an area that is away from direct heat and light.

Fair Isle

This technique, used to make patterns with several colors, involves stranding two or more colors per row. To keep tension even and prevent holes in your knitting, pick up yarns alternately over and under one another, across or around. To keep your work from puckering, stretch the stitches on the needle while you knit, so that they are a bit wider than the length of the float at the back of the garment.

Gauge

It is important to knit a gauge swatch before beginning any project, especially if you are knitting garments; otherwise, the garments simply won't fit properly. Try using different needle sizes to knit the gauge swatch until the sample measures the required number of stitches and rows in the project. If you want fewer stitches per inch/cm, use larger needles; if you want more stitches per inch/cm, use smaller needles. Keep your gauge swatch for blocking.

Intarsia

This is done using small balls of yarn for individual colors. It is an ideal technique for knitting motifs that are not repeated close together. When changing colors, be sure to pick up the new color and wrap it around the old color to prevent holes.

Sizes

The sizes in these projects should only be used as suggested guidelines, as every child is different. If possible, measure the child you are knitting for before you start knitting, to make sure you select the right size.

Yarns

The yarns listed in these projects are suggestions; feel free to substitute according to your preference, and availability. Remember that you'll need to knit to the given gauge in order to obtain the given measurements with a different yarn, so adjust gauge accordingly. Consider whether you'll need to adjust the quantity of yarn for your project in advance, especially if you are ordering your yarn online.

Seams

Woven

This makes an invisible seam between two pieces knitted in Stockinette stitch. With right side (RS) of both pieces facing, line up edges so that they are even and insert needle under horizontal bar in one piece, between first and second stitches. Bring needle up and over, inserting it into corresponding bar on other piece. Pull yarn gently until sides meet. Continue in this manner, alternating from side to side.

Crocheted

This makes a seam between two pieces knitted in any pattern. With wrong side (WS) of both pieces facing, line up edges so that they are even, and insert hook into 2nd stitch in one piece, and into corresponding stitch on other piece. Pull yarn through and slip stitch through both pieces along edge until sides meet. Fasten off.

Terms and Abbreviations

approx approximately

beg begin

BO bind off–Lift first stitch over second, second over third, etc. to finish an edge and keep stitches from unraveling

ch chain stitch

CO cast on–A foundation of stitches placed on needle to begin knitting

cont continue

cm centimeters

C6B sl 3 sts onto cable needle, move to back of work, k next 3 sts, k3 sts from cable needle

C6F sl 3 sts onto cable needle, move to front of work, k next 3 sts, k3 sts from cable needle

C9B sl 3 sts onto cable needle, move to back of work, k next 3 sts, k3 sts from cable needle, k next 3 sts

C9F k3 sts, sl next 3 sts onto cable needle, move to front of work, k next 3 sts, k3 sts from cable needle

dec decrease–Reduce stitches in a row by knitting 2 together

dec 1 st each side K2, k2tog, k to last 4 sts, skp, k to end

dpn double pointed needles

g grams

garter stitch Knit every row

inc increase

inc 1 st each side K2, inc 1, k to last 3 sts, inc 1, k to end

k or K knit

k2tog knit 2 stitches together

m meter

MC Main color

mm millimeter

oz ounce

p or P purl

p2tog purl 2 stitches together

pat pattern

pick up and k Knit into loops along an edge

psso pass slip stitch over

prev previous

rem remaining

rep repeat

rib vertical columns of side-by-side knit and purl stitches

rnd(s) round (s)

RS right side

sc single crochet

sk skip

sl st slip stitch

skp slip 1, knit 1, pass slipped stitch over knit 1

sl slip

St st Stockinette stitch–Knit right side rows, purl wrong side rows. In circular knitting, knit all rows

st(s) stitches

tog together

WS wrong side

work even Continue according to garment shape

yd yard

yo yarn over

* repeat instructions following the single asterisk as many times as written

( ) work enclosed instructions as many times as specified for each size

❀ Techniques ❀

Pompons

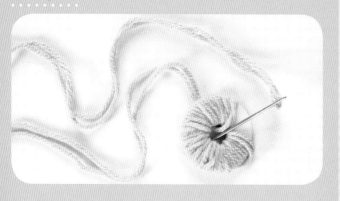

Copy appropriate disk template onto tracing paper. Cut out and transfer twice to cardboard; then cut out two cardboard disks.

Lay the cardboard disks on top of each other so that the holes in the centers are lined up. Thread needle with 2 strands of yarn, and wrap the disks by drawing the thread up through the holes in the center of the disks, and around the disks' outer edge. Wrap the yarn snuggly, so that the strands sit close together, until the hole is filled.

Insert the scissors between the disks and cut the yarn all around. Cut a 39"/1m piece of yarn and tie tightly around the middle of the pompon, between the disks. Cut the yarn, leaving 20"/50cm tails for attaching the pompon.

Remove the cardboard disks and trim the yarn to make the pompon even. Fluff up with a little steam.

Stitches

Simple cables

Crossing to the right using 6 stitches (C6B)

1. On right side (RS) row, work to beginning of cable, then slip next 3 stitches onto cable needle and hold at back of work.
2. Knit next 3 stitches, pulling yarn tightly so that there is no gap.
3. Knit 3 stitches from cable needle.
4. Continue in Stockinette St on 6 cable stitches until you reach next cable row.

Crossing to the left using 6 stitches (C6F)

Work as above, but hold cable needle at front of work instead of back.

Crochet stitches

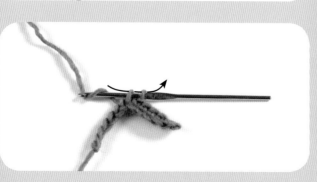

Chain stitch

1. Make a slipknot.
2. Yarn over, pull yarn through loop on hook.
3. Repeat step 2 to make a chain.

Slip stitch

1. Insert hook into a stitch in garment, yarn over and pull yarn through.
2. Insert hook into next stitch, yarn over, and pull yarn through both stitch and loop on hook.
3. Continue in this manner, inserting hook into each stitch.

Single crochet

1. Insert hook into a stitch, yarn over and pull yarn through stitch.
2. Insert hook into next stitch, yarn over and pull yarn through stitch. Now there are two loops on hook.
3. Yarn over, and pull yarn through both loops on hook.
4. Repeat steps 2 and 3.

Sewing and Embroidery stitches

Whip stitch

This is a simple over-and-over stitch that is used to connect two pieces together to form a hem or seam.

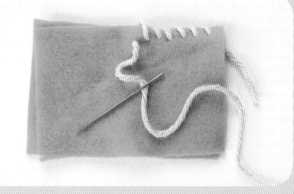

Running stitch

In this stitch, the thread runs in a single direction without doubling back. Surface stitches should be of equal length. This stitch can be used to hold two pieces together, or to embroider a single piece.

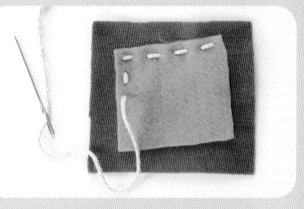

Satin stitch

Bring needle up through fabric, and make a single stitch. Bring needle up again very close to beginning of previous stitch, and repeat.

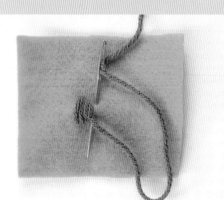

Purple Polka Dot Coat

With polka dots on the cuffs, collar, waist, and strap, this coat blends
classic style with adorable accents.

EXPERIENCE LEVEL

■■■□ Intermediate

SIZES

Sized for 12 (18, 24) months. Shown in size 12 months.

FINISHED MEASUREMENTS

Chest at underarm 23 (25, 27)"/58.5 (63.5, 68.5)cm

Length 11 (13, 15)"/28 (33, 38)cm

Sleeve width at upper arm 12 (12½, 13)"/30.5 (31.5, 33)cm

MATERIALS AND TOOLS

Yarn A (SUPER BULKY 6): 370yd/338m of Bulky weight yarn, acrylic/polyester, in violet with dark blue and gray

Yarn B (SUPER BULKY 6): 153yd/140 m of Bulky weight yarn, acrylic/wool, in purple

Yarn C: 185yd/169 m of Bulky weight yarn, acrylic/polyester, in variegated blue and lavender

Size 8 (5 mm) straight knitting needles OR SIZE TO OBTAIN GAUGE

Size H/8 (5mm) crochet hook

Stitch holder

Six ¾"/2cm buttons

Yarn needle

GAUGE

With Yarn B, in St st, 14 sts and 20 rows to 4"/10cm

With Yarn A, in Garter st, 14 sts and 24 rows to 4"/10cm

Measurements

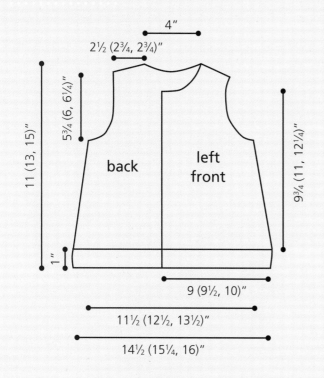

4"

2½ (2¾, 2¾)"

5¾ (6, 6¼)"

11 (13, 15)"

9¾ (11, 12¼)"

back

left front

1"

9 (9½, 10)"

11½ (12½, 13½)"

14½ (15¼, 16)"

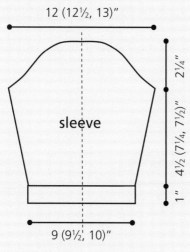

12 (12½, 13)"

sleeve

2¼"

4½ (7¼, 7½)"

1"

9 (9½, 10)"

Polka Dot Pattern

row
2
1
sts 4 3 2 1

Color and stitch key:

Yarn C ■ : K on RS rows and P on WS rows

Yarn B ■ : K on RS rows and P on WS rows

Instructions

BACK

With Yarn B, cast on 52 (56, 60) sts.

Work in St st for 2 rows.

BEG POLKA DOT PATTERN

Pat consists of 4 sts and 2 rows.

Work 3 sts in St st, *work in Polka Dot Pattern on 4 sts, rep from * 12 (13, 14) times; work in St st to end.

Cont as established for 2 rows.

Work in St st for 2 more rows.

Cut Yarn B.

Join Yarn A.

Work in Garter st for 36 (42, 48) rows, dec 1 st each side every 6th row 6 (7, 8) times—40 (42, 44) sts.

ARMHOLE SHAPING

Rows 1–2: Bind off 2 (2, 3) sts, k to end.

Rows 3–4: Bind off 2 sts, k to end.

Rows 5–6: Bind off 1 st, k to end.

Work in Garter st for 20 (22, 24) rows—30 (32, 32) sts.

End with WS row.

SHOULDERS AND BACK NECK SHAPING

Row 1: Bind off 5 (6, 6) sts for right shoulder, k4, bind off center 10 sts for neck, k to end.

Work each shoulder separately.

Leave rem 5 sts for right shoulder on a holder.

LEFT SHOULDER

Row 2: Bind off 5 (6, 6) sts, k to end.

Row 3: K all sts.

Row 4: Bind off rem 5 sts.

RIGHT SHOULDER

With RS facing, rejoin yarn to rem sts.

Rows 2–3: K all sts.

Row 4: Bind off rem 5 sts.

LEFT FRONT

With Yarn B, cast on 32 (34, 36) sts.

Work in St st for 2 rows.

BEG POLKA DOT PATTERN

Work 3 (2, 3) st in St st, *work in Polka Dot Pattern on 4 sts, rep from * 7 (8, 8) times; work in St st to end.

Cont as established for 2 rows.

Work in St st for 2 more rows.

Cut Yarn B.

Join Yarn A.

Work in Garter st for 36 (42, 48) rows, dec 1 st at the end of every 6th row (WS Row) 6 (7, 8) times—26 (27, 28) sts.

End with WS row.

ARMHOLE SHAPING

Row 1: Bind off 2 (2, 3) sts, k to end.

Row 2 and all WS rows: K all sts.

Row 3: Bind off 2 sts, k to end.

Row 5: Bind off 1 st, k to end.

Work in Garter st for 18 (20, 22) rows—21 (22, 22) sts.

End with WS row.

SHOULDERS AND FRONT NECK SHAPING

Row 1: K all sts.

Row 2: Bind off 5 sts for neck, k to end.

Row 3: Bind off 5 (6, 6) sts for shoulder, k to end.

Row 4: Bind off 3 sts for neck, k to end.

Row 5: Bind off 5 sts for shoulder, k to end.

Row 6: Bind off rem 3 sts for neck.

RIGHT FRONT

Work as for left front until Garter st pat begins.

Work in Garter st for 36 (42, 48) rows, dec 1 st at beg of every 6th (WS) row 6 (7, 8) times —26 (27, 28) sts, and making buttonholes as follows:

Row 1: K all sts.

Buttonhole rows

Row 2 (WS): K to last 5 sts, bind off 2 sts, k2.

Row 3: K3, cast on 2 sts, k to end.

Work buttonholes rows from 2nd and every following 20th (22th, 24th) row 4 times.

ARMHOLE, SHOULDER, AND FRONT NECK SHAPING

Work to correspond to left front, reversing shaping and making buttonholes when necessary.

SLEEVES

With Yarn B, cast on 32 (34, 36) sts.

Work in St st for 2 rows.

BEG POLKA DOT PATTERN

Work 3 (2, 3) st in St st, *work in Polka Dot Pattern on 4 sts, rep from * 7 (8, 8) times; work in St st to end.

Cont as established for 2 rows.

Work in St st for 2 more rows.

Cut Yarn B.

Join Yarn A.

Work in Garter st for 30 (40, 40) rows, inc 1 st each side every 6th (8th, 8th) row 5 times—42 (44, 46) sts.

SLEEVE TOP SHAPING

Bind off 2 sts at beg of next 6 rows; work in Garter st to end.

Bind off 1 st at beg of next 4 rows; work in Garter st to end.

Bind off 2 sts at beg of next 2 rows; work in Garter st to end.

Bind off 3 sts at beg of next 2 rows; work in Garter st to end—16 (18, 20) sts.

Bind off rem sts.

BACK STRAP

With Yarn B, cast on 20 sts.

Work in St st for 2 rows.

BEG POLKA DOT PATTERN

Work 3 sts in St st, *work in Polka Dot Pattern on 4 sts, rep from * 4 times; work in St st to end.

Cont as established for 2 rows.

Work in St st for 2 more rows.

Bind off all sts.

FINISHING

Sew shoulder seams. Sew side and sleeve seams.

Set in sleeves sewing last ¼"/6mm at top of sleeve to bound-off armhole sts.

Sew on buttons.

COLLAR

With RS facing and Yarn B, starting at 3rd st from corner of right front neck, pick up and k48 (52, 56) sts across to 3rd st from corner of left front neck.

*Row 1: P3, work in k2, p2 rib to last 5 sts, k2, p3.

Row 2: K3, work in p2, k2 rib to last 5 sts, p2, k3.

Rep from * 4 (5, 5) times.

Work in St st for 2 (2, 4) rows.

BEG POLKA DOT PATTERN

Work 3 sts in St st, *work in Polka Dot Pattern on 4 sts, rep from * 11 (12, 13) times, work in St st to end.

Cont as established for 2 rows.

Work in St st for 2 more rows.

Bind off loosely all sts.

CROCHETED EDGING

With RS facing and Yarn C, insert hook in bottom corner of left front.

Ch 1, then sc 1 evenly across bottom to right front corner, sc 3 into corner, cont along right front edge up to top right front corner, sc 3 into corner, cont to right bottom corner of collar. End with sl st.

Work same for sleeve edgings. Join with sl st and fasten off.

CROCHETED COLLAR EDGING

With WS facing and Yarn C, insert hook into bottom left corner of coll ar.

Ch 1, then sc 1 evenly across collar edge to right bottom corner of collar. Sc 3 into each top corner. End with sl st.

CROCHETED STRAP

With RS facing and Yarn C, insert hook into a strap corner, ch 1, sc 1 evenly across strap edge. Sc 3 into each corner. Join with sl st and fasten off.

Sew strap on back, middle, then sew buttons on each end.

This project was knit with

(A) 2 balls of Lion Homespun, 98% acrylic/2% polyester, bulky weight, 6oz/170g = approx 185yd/169m per ball, color #790-336

(B) 1 ball of Lion Wool-Ease Chunky, 80% acrylic/20% wool, bulky weight, 5oz/140g = approx 153yd/140m per ball, color #630-146

(C) 1 ball of Lion Homespun, 98% acrylic/2% polyester, bulky weight, 6oz/170g = approx 185yd/169m, color #790-341

Best Friend Cardigan

Girls will love having a little braided friend on the back of their cardigan. The front of this design features pretty pink buttons and two small pockets for storing treasures.

EXPERIENCE LEVEL

■■■□ Intermediate

SIZES

Sized for 12 (18, 24) months. Shown in size 18 months.

FINISHED MEASUREMENTS

Chest at underarm 24 (26, 28)"/61 (66, 71)cm

Length 11 (12, 13)"/28 (30.5, 33)cm

Upper arm 9½ (10, 10½)"/24 (25.5, 27)cm

MATERIALS AND TOOLS

Yarn A (6 SUPER BULKY): 363yd/330m of Bulky weight yarn, acrylic/wool, in pale green

Yarn B (6 SUPER BULKY): 121yd/110m of Bulky weight yarn, acrylic/wool, in variegated pink, gray and white

Size 10 (6mm) straight knitting needles OR SIZE TO OBTAIN GAUGE

Size 8 (5mm) circular knitting needle OR SIZE TO OBTAIN GAUGE

Size E/4 (3.5mm) crochet hook

Stitch holder

Four ⅝"/13mm buttons

Yarn needle

GAUGE

In St st, 16 sts and 21 rows to 4"/10cm

Measurements

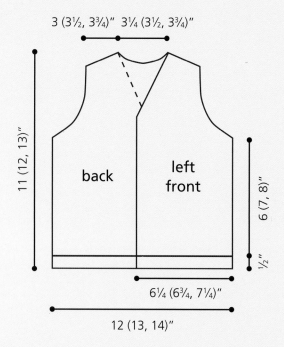

3 (3½, 3¾)" 3¼ (3½, 3¾)"

11 (12, 13)"

back

left front

6 (7, 8)"

½"

6¼ (6¾, 7¼)"

12 (13, 14)"

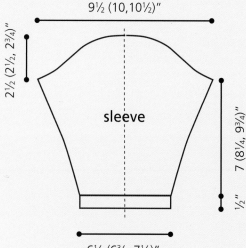

9½ (10, 10½)"

2½ (2½, 2¾)"

sleeve

7 (8¼, 9¾)"

½"

6¼ (6¾, 7¼)"

Instructions

BACK

With straight needles and Yarn B, cast on 47 (51, 55) sts.

Work in k1, p1 rib for 3 rows. Cut Yarn B.

Join Yarn A. Work in St st for 8 (12, 16) rows. End with a WS row.

BEG LITTLE GIRL PATTERN

Pat consists of 21 sts and 30 rows.

Work 13 (15, 17) sts in St st, work in pat on 21 middle sts, work in St st to end.

Cont as established through pat row 24.

ARMHOLE SHAPING

Row 1: Bind off 2 sts, k across 10 (12, 14) sts, work pat row 25 over next 21 sts, k to end.

Row 2: Bind off 2 sts, p across 10 (12, 14) sts, work pat row 26 over next 21 sts, p to end.

Row 3: Bind off 1st, k across 9 (11, 13) sts, work pat row 27 over next 21 sts, k to end.

Row 4: Bind off 1st, p across 9 (11, 13) sts, work pat row 28 over next 21 sts, p to end.

Row 5: Bind off 1st, k across 8 (10, 12) sts, work pat row 29 over next 21 sts, k to end.

Row 6: Bind off 1st, p across 8 (10, 12) sts, work pat row 30 over next 21 sts, p to end.

Row 7—8: Bind off 1st, work across in St st.

Cont to work in St st for 14(16, 18) more rows.

SHOULDERS AND BACK NECK SHAPING

Row 1: Bind off 6 (6, 7) sts for right shoulder, k5 (7, 7), bind off center 13 (13, 15) sts for neck, k to end.

Work each shoulder and each side of neck separately.

Leave rem sts for right shoulder on a holder.

LEFT SHOULDER

Row 2: Bind off 6 (6, 7) sts for shoulder, p to end.

Row 3: Bind off 1 (2, 2) sts for neck, k to end.

Row 4: Bind off last 5 (6, 6) sts for shoulder.

RIGHT SHOULDER

With RS facing, rejoin yarn to rem sts.

Row 2: K all sts.

Row 3: Bind off 1 (2, 2) sts for neck, p to end.

Row 4: Bind off last 5 (6, 6) sts for shoulder.

LEFT FRONT

With straight needles and Yarn B, cast on 25 (27, 29) sts.

Work in k1, p1 rib for 3 rows. Cut Yarn B.

Join Yarn A. Work in St st for 32 (36, 40) rows. End with a WS row.

ARMHOLE SHAPING

Row 1: Bind off 2 sts, k to end.

Row 2: P all sts.

*Row 3: Bind off 1st, k to end.

Row 4: P all sts.

Rep from * 3 times.

LEFT SHOULDER AND FRONT NECK SHAPING

*Row 1(RS): K all sts.

Row 2: Bind off 1 st, p to end

Rep from * 7 (8, 9) times.

Row 15 (17, 19): Bind off 6 (6, 7) sts for shoulder, k to end.

Row 16 (18, 20): Bind off 1 st for neck, p to end.

Row 17 (19, 21): Bind off 5 (6, 6) sts for shoulder, k1.

Row 18 (20, 22): Bind off last 1 st for neck.

RIGHT FRONT

Work as for left front until armhole shaping begins.

ARMHOLE SHAPING

Row 1: K all sts.

Row 2: Bind off 2 sts, p to end.

*Row 3: K all sts.

Row 4: Bind off 1sts, p to end.

Rep from * 3 times.

RIGHT SHOULDER AND FRONT NECK SHAPING

*Row 1 (RS): Bind off 1 st, k to end

Row 2: P all sts.

Rep from * 7 (8, 9) times.

Row 15 (17, 19): Bind off 1 st for neck, k to end.

Row 16 (18, 20): Bind off 6 (6, 7) sts for shoulder, p to end.

Row 17 (19,21): Bind off 1 st for neck, k to end.

Row 17 (20, 22): Bind off last 5 (6, 6) sts for shoulder.

SLEEVES

With straight needles and Yarn B, cast on 25 (27, 29) sts.

Work in k1, p1 rib for 3 rows. Cut Yarn B.

Join Yarn A. Work in St st, inc 1 st at each side of next and every following 6th row 6 (7, 8) times—37 (41, 45) sts.

SLEEVE TOP SHAPING

Bind off 2 (3, 3) sts at beg of next 2 rows work in St st to end.

Bind off 2 sts at beg of next 2 rows; work in St st to end.

Bind off 1 st at beg of next 6 (6, 8) rows; work in St st to end.

Bind off 2 sts at beg of next 2 rows; work in St st to end.

Bind off 3 sts at beg of next 2 rows; work in St st to end—13 (15, 17) sts.

Bind off rem sts.

POCKETS

(Make 2)

With RS of front facing, bottom away from you, Yarn A and sraight knitting needles, pick up and k13 (13, 15) center sts, inserting needle through 5th row sts above ribbing.

Work in St st for 7 (7, 9) more rows, beg with p row. Cut Yarn A.

Join Yarn B. Work in k1, p1 rib for 3 rows.

Bind off all sts in rib pat.

FINISHING

Trace legs, arms, and head shapes using brown part of Yarn B with Running stitch.

BRAIDS

(Make 2)

Insert hook through st where you want braid to begin, fold pink part of Yarn B in half, pull yarn through, and with 2 strands, ch 7. Cut Yarn B and tie.

Using hook and Yarn A, sew in right and left edges of pocket as follows: Sl st through second st from left and right pocket edge st and corresponding cardigan st, folding edge sts under pocket.

Sew shoulder seams. Sew side and sleeve seams.

Set in sleeves sewing last ¼"/6mm at top of sleeve to bound-off armhole sts.

BORDER

With RS facing, Yarn B, and circular needle, starting at bottom corner of right front, pick up and K46 (52, 58) sts up right front border to right shoulder seam, then 19 (21, 23) sts across back neck opening to left shoulder seam, then 46 (52, 58) sts down left front border to bottom corner of left front—111 (125, 139) sts

Row 1(WS): P1, work in k1, p1 rib to end.

Buttonhole rows

Row 2: Work in k1, p1 rib to last 30 (34,38) sts. *Bind off 1 st, rib 4 (5, 6). Rep from * 4 times, bind off 1 st, rib to end.

Row 3: Rib back, casting on 1 st over this bind off st on previous row.

Row 4: K1, work in p1, k1 rib to end.

Bind off all sts in rib pat.

This project was knit with

(A) 3 balls of Patons Shetland Chunky, 75% acrylic/25% wool yarn, bulky weight, 3½oz/100g = approx 121yd/110m per ball, color #03240

(B) 1 ball Patons Shetland Chunky, 75% acrylic/25% wool yarn, bulky weight, 3½oz/100g = approx 121yd/110m per ball, color #03425

Color and stitch key:
Yarn A ▨ : K on RS rows and P on WS rows
Yarn A ▨ : P on RS rows and K on WS rows
Yarn B ■ : P on RS rows and K on WS rows

Little Girl Pattern

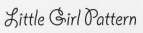
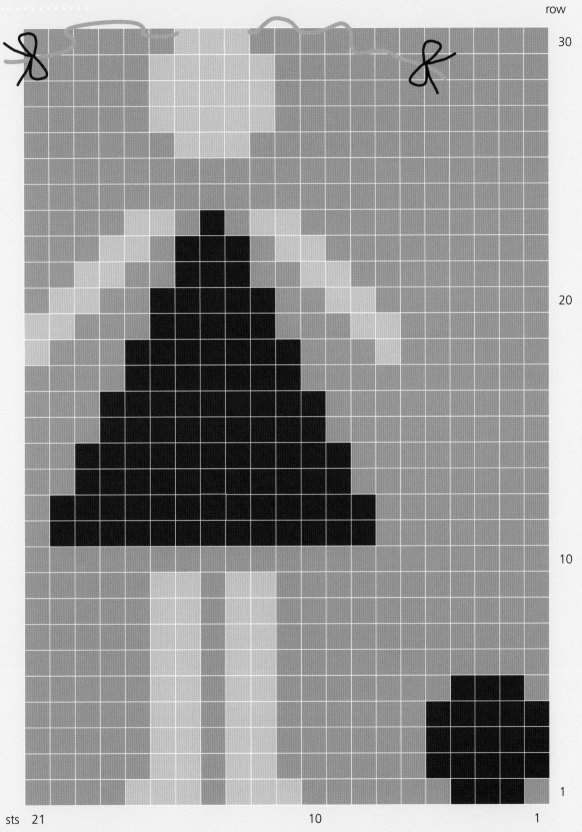

30

20

10

1

sts 21   10   1

Garden of Delight Pullover

The flowers on this pretty pullover won't ever wilt, so you know your little flower will always be in good company. Perfect for little people who love playing in the garden.

EXPERIENCE LEVEL

▬ ▬ ▬ ▭ Intermediate

SIZES

Sized for 12 (18, 24) months. Shown in size 18 months.

FINISHED MEASUREMENTS

Chest at underarm 21 (23, 25)"/56 (58.5, 63.5)cm

Length 12½ (13, 14¾)"/32 (33, 37.5)cm

Sleeve width at upper arm 11 (11½, 12)"/28 (29, 30.5)cm

MATERIALS AND TOOLS

Yarn A **MEDIUM 4**: 394yd/360m of Medium weight yarn, acrylic/wool, in deep purple

Yarn B **MEDIUM 4**: 197yd/180m of Medium weight yarn, acrylic/wool, in light pink

Yarn C **SUPER BULKY 6**: 122yd/110 m of Bulky weight yarn, polyester, in green

Size 8 (5mm) straight knitting needles OR SIZE TO OBTAIN GAUGE

Size E/4 (3.5mm) crochet hook

Stitch holder

Three ⅝"/13mm buttons

Two ⁵⁄₁₆"/7mm paillettes

Yarn needle

Elastic string

GAUGE

In St st, 19 sts and 24 rows to 4"/10cm

In Seed st, 19 sts and 32 rows to 4"/10cm

Measurements

SEED ST

Row 1: *K1, p1; rep from * to end.

Row 2: K the purl sts and p the knit sts.

Rep rows 1 and 2 for pat.

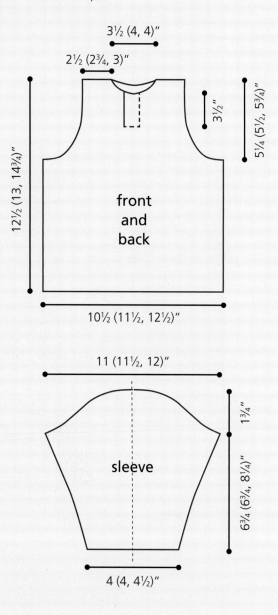

Instructions

FRONT

With Yarn B, cast on 56 (60, 64) sts.

Work in St st for 3 (3, 5) rows.

Work in Garter st for 3 rows.

Cut Yarn B.

Join Yarn A. Work in St st for 2 rows.

Work in Seed st for 8 (8, 12) rows.

Work in St st for 2 (2, 4) rows.

BEG FLOWERS PATTERN

Pat consists of 16 sts and 25 rows.

*Row 1 (RS): K32 (36, 40), work in Flowers Pattern on 16 sts, k to end.

Row 2: P8, work in pat on 16 sts, p to end.

Rep from * 12 times.

Rep row 1 once more. End with RS row.

Work in St st for 3 (3, 5) rows. End with WS row.

ARMHOLE SHAPING

Bind off 2 (2, 3) sts at beg of next 2 rows; work in Garter st to end.

Bind off 2 sts at beg of next 2 rows; work in Garter st to end.

Cut Yarn A.

Join Yarn B. Bind off 1 st at beg of next 2 rows; work in St st to end.

Bind off 1 st at beg of next 2 rows; work in Seed st to end—44 (48, 50) sts.

Cont to work in Seed st for 12 (14, 16) more rows.

LEFT FRONT NECK SHAPING

Work on first 26 (28, 28) sts, place rem sts onto holder.

Row 1: Work in Seed st to last 4 sts, k to end.

Row 2: K4, work in Seed st to end.

Rows 3-6: Rep rows 1 and 2 two more times.

Buttonhole rows

Row 7: Work in Seed st to last 4 sts, k1, bind off 1, k1.

Row 8: K2, cast on 1, k1; work in Seed st to end.

Rows 9-12: *Rep rows 1 and 2 two more times.

Rows 13 and14: Work buttonhole rows 7 and 8.

Rows 15-20: Rep rows 9-12 and 13 and 14 once more.

Rows 21, 23, 25 and 27: Work in Seed st.

Row 22: Bind off 7 (8, 7) sts; work in Seed st to end.

Row 24 and 26: Bind off 3 sts; work in Seed st to end.

Row 28: Bind off 13 (14, 15) sts for shoulder.

RIGHT FRONT NECK SHAPING

Place last 18 (20, 22) sts from holder back onto needle.

Note: When changing colors, twist yarns tog on WS to prevent holes.

Row 1 (RS): With Yarn A, k4; with Yarn B, work in Seed st to end.

Row 2: With Yarn B, work in Seed st to last 4 sts; with Yarn A, k to end.

Rows 3-24: Rep rows 1 and 2, 11 times more.

Row 25: With Yarn A, bind off 2 (3, 4) sts; with Yarn B, work in Seed st to end. Cut Yarn A.

Row 26: With Yarn B, work in Seed st.

Row 27: Bind off 3 sts, work in Seed st to end

Row 28: Bind off 13 (14, 15) sts for shoulder.

BACK

With Yarn B, cast on 56 (60, 64) sts.

Work in St st for 3 (3, 5) rows.

Work in Garter st for 3 rows.

Cut Yarn B.

Join Yarn A. Work in St st for 2 rows.

Work in Seed st for 8 (8, 12) rows.

Work in St st for 30 (30, 34) rows.

ARMHOLE SHAPING

Bind off 2 (2, 3) sts at beg of next 2 rows; work in Garter st to end.

Bind off 2 sts at beg of next 2 rows; work in Garter st to end.

Cut Yarn A.

Join Yarn B. Bind off 1 st at beg of next 2 rows; work in St st to end.

Bind off 1 st at beg of next 2 rows; work in Seed st to end—44 (48, 50) sts.

Cont to work in Seed st for 34 (36, 38) more rows.

BACK NECK SHAPING

Row 1: Work in Seed st on 16 (18, 18) sts, bind off center

12 (12, 14) sts for neck, work in Seed st to end.

Work each side of neck separately.

Leave rem sts for right neck on a holder.

LEFT BACK NECK SHAPING

Rows 2 and 4 (WS): Work in Seed st.

Row 3: Bind off 2 sts; work in Seed st to end.

Row 5: Bind off 1 (2, 1) sts; work in Seed st to end.

Bind off 13 (14, 15) sts for shoulder.

RIGHT BACK NECK SHAPING

Rows 2 and 4 (RS): Work in Seed st.

Row 3: Bind off 2 sts; work in Seed st to end.

Row 5: Bind off 1 (2, 1) sts; work in Seed st to end.

Bind off 13 (14, 15) sts for shoulder.

SLEEVES

With Yarn B, cast on 40 (40, 42) sts.

Work in St st for 3 (3, 5) rows.

Work in Garter st for 3 rows.

Cut Yarn B.

Join Yarn A.

Next Row: K0 (0, 1), *k3, inc1; rep from * 5 times, *inc1, k3; rep from * 5 times, K0 (0, 1)—50 (50, 52) sts.

Work in p for 1 row.

Work in Seed st for 8 (8, 12) rows.

Work in St st for 30 (30, 34) rows, inc 1 st at each side of 9th (9th, 11th) and 29th (29th, 31st) rows—54 (54, 56) sts.

SLEEVE TOP SHAPING

Bind off 2 sts at beg of next 2 rows; work in Garter st to end.

Bind off 1 (1, 2) sts at beg of next 2 rows; work in Garter st to end.

Cut Yarn A.

Join Yarn B. Bind off 1 st at beg of next 2 rows; work in St st to end.

Bind off 1 st at beg of next 2 rows; work in Seed st to end.

Bind off 2 sts at beg of next 2 rows; work in Seed st to end.

Bind off 3 sts at beg of next 4 rows; work in Seed st to end—28 sts.

Bind off rem sts.

FINISHING

Sew shoulder seams. Sew side and sleeve seams. Set in sleeves sewing last ⅕"/5mm at top of sleeve to bound-off armhole sts.

Sew on buttons. Sew paillettes on flowers centers.

With WS facing, using yarn needle and elastic string, loosely weave string through knots of last rows of Garter sts all around bottom of sleeves, top of sleeves, bottom of pullover, and chest.

CROCHETED EDGING

With RS facing, front facing, bottom at your right, and Yarn A, insert needle into top corner of right neck opening, ch 1, *ch 3, sl st in first ch, sc 1 in next st. Rep from * all around neck opening and down along left front border. End with sl st and fasten off.

This project was knit with

(A) 2 balls of Lion Wool-Ease, 80% acrylic/20% wool yarn, medium weight, 3oz/85g = approx 197yd/180m per ball, color #620-139

(B) 1 ball of Lion Wool-Ease, 80% acrylic/20% wool yarn, medium weight, 3oz/85g = approx 197yd/180m per ball, color #620-104

(C) 1 ball of Lion Suede, 100% polyester yarn, bulky weight, 3oz/85g = approx 122yd/110m per ball, color #210-132

Flowers Pattern

Color and stitch key:

Yarn A ▉ : K on RS rows and P on WS rows
Yarn B ▉ : K on RS rows and P on WS rows
Yarn C ▉ : K on RS rows and P on WS rows

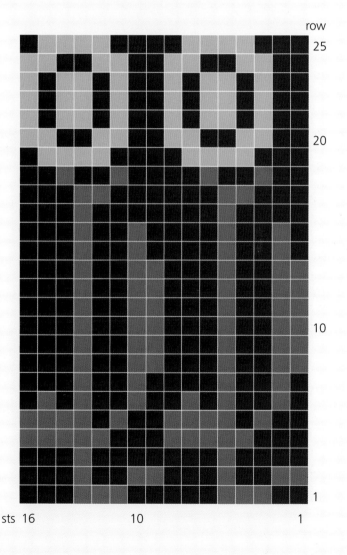

Forest Cardigan

With a range of rich browns and a forest green trim, this cardigan is perfect for keeping young adventurers warm when they wander on cool autumn mornings.

EXPERIENCE LEVEL

■■■☐ Intermediate

SIZES

Sized for 12 (18, 24) months. Shown in size 24 months.

FINISHED MEASUREMENTS

Chest at underarm 23 (25, 27)"/58.5 (63.5, 68.5)cm

Length 12½ (13, 14¾)"/32 (33, 37.5)cm

Upper arm 9 (10, 11")/22 (25.5, 28)cm

MATERIALS AND TOOLS

For boys

Yarn A **SUPER BULKY 6** : 363yd/330m of Bulky weight yarn, acrylic/wool, in brown, green, and gray

Yarn B **SUPER BULKY 6** : 121yd/110m of Bulky weight yarn, acrylic/wool, in brown

Yarn C **SUPER BULKY 6** : 153yd/140m of Bulky weight yarn, acrylic/wool, in green

For girls

Yarn A **SUPER BULKY 6** : 363yd/330m of Bulky weight yarn, acrylic/wool, in light green, brown and white

Yarn B **SUPER BULKY 6** : 121yd/110m of Bulky weight yarn, acrylic/wool, in light green

Yarn C **SUPER BULKY 6** : 153yd/140m of Bulky weight yarn, acrylic/wool, in green

Sizes 10 (6mm) and 8 (5mm) straight knitting needles OR SIZES TO OBTAIN GAUGE

Size H/8 (5 mm) crochet hook

Five ¾"/2cm buttons

Yarn needle

GAUGE

With larger needles, in St st, 16 sts and 21 rows to 4"/10cm

Measurements

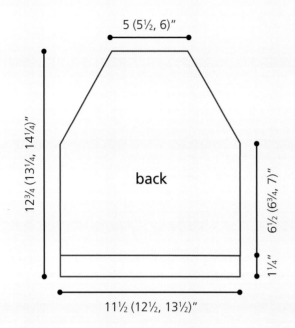

5 (5½, 6)"

12¾ (13¼, 14¼)"

back

6½ (6¾, 7)"

1¼"

11½ (12½, 13½)"

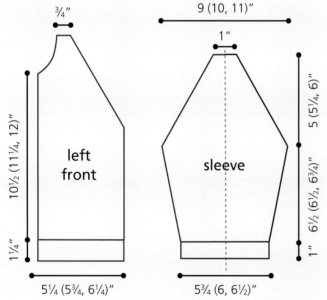

¾"

left front

10½ (11¼, 12)"

1¼"

5¼ (5¾, 6¼)"

9 (10, 11)"

1"

sleeve

5 (5¼, 6)"

6½ (6½, 6¾)"

1"

5¾ (6, 6½)"

Instructions

BACK

Note: Purl side is RS of garment for Rev St st.

With larger needles and Yarn B, cast on 48 (52, 56) sts.

*Row 1 (WS row): P3, work in k2, p2 rib to last 5 sts, k2, p3.

Row 2: K3, work in p2, k2 rib to last 5 sts, p2, k3.

Rep from * 3 times.

Rep row 1 once.

Next row (RS row): P all sts. Cut Yarn B.

Join Yarn A. Work in Rev St st, for 31 (33, 35) rows, beginning on WS with k row. End with a WS row.

RAGLAN ARMHOLES SHAPING

*Row 1: P all sts.

Row 2 (WS): K2, k2tog, k across to last 4 sts, skp, k to end.

Rep from * 14 (15, 16) times, total—20 (22, 24) sts.

Bind off in purl rem 20 (22, 24) sts.

LEFT FRONT

With larger needles and Yarn B, cast on 22 (24, 26) sts.

Beg with WS row, work in k2, p2 rib for 7 rows.

Next row (RS row): P all sts. Cut Yarn B.

Join Yarn A. Work in Rev St st for 31 (33, 35) rows, beginning on WS with k row. End with a WS row.

RAGLAN ARMHOLE AND FRONT NECK SHAPING

*Row 1: P all sts.

Row 2 (WS): K across to last 4 sts, skp, k to end.

Rep from * 11 (12, 13) times, total—11 (12, 13) sts.

Row 23 (25, 27) and all RS rows: P all sts.

Row 24 (26, 28): Bind off 2 (2, 3) sts for neck, k across to last 4 sts, skp, k to end.

Row 26 (28, 30): Bind off 2 sts for neck, k across to last 4 sts, skp, k to end.

Row 28 (30, 32): Bind off 1 (2, 2) sts for neck, k across to last 4 sts, skp, k to end.

Bind off in p rem 3 sts.

RIGHT FRONT

With larger needles and Yarn B, cast on 22 (24, 26) sts.

Beg with WS row, work in p2, k2 rib for 7 rows.

Next row (RS row): P all sts. Cut Yarn B.

Join Yarn A. Work in Rev St st for 31 (33, 35) rows, beginning with k row. End with a WS row.

RAGLAN ARMHOLE AND FRONT NECK SHAPING

*Row 1: P all sts.

Row 2 (WS): K2, k2tog, k to end.

Rep from * 11 (12, 13) times, total—11 (12, 13) sts.

Row 23 (25, 27): Bind off 2 (2, 3) sts for neck, p across to end.

Row 24 (26, 28) and all WS rows: K2, k2tog, k across to end.

Row 25 (27, 29): Bind off 2 sts for neck, p across to end.

Row 27 (29, 31): Bind off 1 (2, 2) sts for neck, p across to end.

Bind off in p rem 3 sts.

SLEEVES

With larger needles and Yarn B, cast on 24 (26, 28) sts.

Beg with WS row, work in k2, p2 rib for 5 rows.

Next row (RS row): P all sts. Cut Yarn B.

Join Yarn A. Work in Rev St st, for 4 (6, 8) rows, beginning with k row. End with a RS row.

Cont to work in St st, inc 1 st at each side of next and every following 10th row 3 more times—32 (34, 36) sts. End with WS row.

RAGLAN SHAPING

*Row 1: P all sts.

Row 2 (WS): K2, k2tog, k across to last 4 sts, skp, k to end.

Rep from * 14 (15, 16) times, total—4 sts.

Bind off in p rem 4 sts.

POCKETS

(Make 2)

Note: Knit side is RS of pocket for St st.

With larger needles and Yarn A, cast on 14 (16, 16) sts.

Work in St st for 10 (12, 12) rows, beg with p row. Cut Yarn A.

Join Yarn B. Work in k1, p1 rib for 5 rows.

Bind off all sts in rib pat.

RIGHT FRONT BORDER

With RS facing, Yarn C and smaller needles, start at bottom corner of right front, pick up and K 63 (67, 71) sts up right front border to right front neck.

Work in k1, p1 rib for 4 rows.

Bind off all sts in rib pat.

LEFT FRONT BORDER

With WS facing, Yarn B, and smaller needles, starting at bottom corner of left front, pick up and k63 (67, 71) sts up left front border to left front neck.

Row 1: Work in k1, p1 rib to end.

Buttonhole rows

Row 2: P1, k1, bind off 2 sts, *rib 11 (12, 13), bind off 2 sts. Rep from * 4 times, rib to end.

Row 3: Rib back, casting on 2 sts over bound-off sts on previous row.

Row 4: Work in p1, k1 rib to end.

Bind off all sts in rib pat.

FINISHING

Crocheted pocket border

With RS facing and Yarn B, insert hook into left top pocket corner, ch 1, sc 1 evenly across pocket edges to right top pocket corner. Sc 3 into each bottom corner. End with sl st.

CROCHETED LEFT FRONT BORDER

With WS facing and Yarn C, insert hook into seam of left front border bottom corner, ch 1. Sc 1 evenly across seam up to left front neck. End with sl st and fasten off.

Attach pockets at center of each front, about 4 rows above bottom ribbing. Using hook and Yarn C, sew pocket linings in place as follows: Sl st under each pocket edge st and corresponding cardigan st.

Sew side and sleeve seams. Set in sleeves sewing through 2nd st from sleeve raglan edge to same sts of armhole raglan.

COLLAR

With RS facing, Yarn B, and larger needles, start at 3rd st from corner of right front neck, pick up, and k42 (44, 46) sts across to 3rd st from corner of left front neck.

Work in k2, p2 rib for 15 rows.

Bind off all sts in rib pat.

CROCHETED COLLAR

With WS facing and Yarn B, insert hook into bottom left corner of collar, ch 1, then sc 1 evenly across collar edge to right bottom corner of collar. Sc 3 into each top corner. End with sl st and fasten off.

This project was knit with

For boys

(A): 3 balls of Patons Shetland Chunky, 75% acrylic/25% wool yarn, bulky weight, 3½ oz/100g = approx 121yd/110m per ball, color #03528

(B): 1 ball of Patons Shetland Chunky, 75% acrylic/25% wool yarn, bulky weight, 3½ oz/100g = approx 121yd/110m per ball, color #03031

(C) 1 ball of Lion Wool-Ease Chunky, 80% acrylic/20% wool yarn, bulky weight, 5oz/140g = approx 153yd/140m per ball, color #630-130

For girls

(A): 3 balls of Patons Shetland Chunky, 75% acrylic/25% wool yarn, bulky weight, 3½ oz/100g = approx 121yd/110m per ball, color #03293

(B): 1 ball of Patons Shetland Chunky, 75% acrylic/25% wool yarn, bulky weight, 3½ oz/100g = approx 121yd/110m per ball, color #03241

(C) 1 ball of Lion Wool-Ease Chunky, 80% acrylic/20% wool yarn, bulky weight, 5oz/140g = approx 153yd/140m per ball, color #630-130

A Vested Interest

This vest is excellent for keeping baby's body protected from winter's chilly winds. With solid colors and a bright plaid design, it's just right for babies who are serious about style.

EXPERIENCE LEVEL

■■■ Experienced

SIZES

Sized for 12-18 (24) months. Shown in size 24 months.

FINISHED MEASUREMENTS

Chest at underarm 23¼ (25)"/59 (63.5)cm

Length 13¾ (15)"/ 35 (38)cm

Width at upper arm 11¼ (12)"/28.5 (30.5)cm

MATERIALS AND TOOLS

For boys

Yarn A **6 SUPER BULKY**: 306yd/280m of Bulky weight yarn, acrylic/wool, in amber

Yarn B **6 SUPER BULKY**: 153yd/140m of Bulky weight yarn, acrylic/wool, in dark gray

Yarn C **6 SUPER BULKY**: 153yd/140m of Bulky weight yarn, acrylic/wool, in green

Yarn D **6 SUPER BULKY**: 153yd/140m of Bulky weight yarn, acrylic/wool, in orange

For girls

Yarn A **6 SUPER BULKY**: 306yd/280m of Bulky weight yarn, acrylic/wool, in dark orange

Yarn B **6 SUPER BULKY**: 153yd/140m of Bulky weight yarn, acrylic/wool, in deep rose

Yarn C **6 SUPER BULKY**: 153yd/140m of Bulky weight yarn, acrylic/wool, in blue-violet

Yarn D **6 SUPER BULKY**: 153yd/140m of Bulky weight yarn, acrylic/wool, in amber

Size 10 (6mm) straight knitting needles OR SIZE TO OBTAIN GAUGE
Size 8 (5mm) circular knitting needle OR SIZE TO OBTAIN GAUGE

Stitch holder

Yarn needle

GAUGE

With larger needles, in St st, 14 sts and 20 rows to 4"/10cm

Measurements

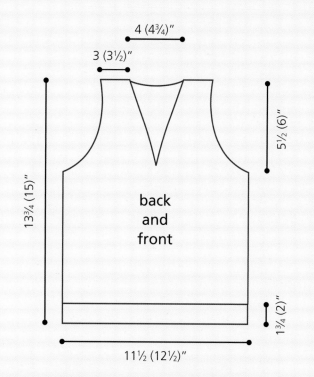

4 (4¾)"

3 (3½)"

13¾ (15)"

5½ (6)"

1¾ (2)"

back and front

11½ (12½)"

Instructions

FRONT

With Yarn B and straight needles, cast on 45 (51) sts.

Work in k3, p3 rib for 8 (10) rows.

Cut Yarn A.

BEG FRONT PLAID PATTERN

Pat consists of 17 sts and 16 rows.

Join Yarn A and work in St st for 14 (17) sts, work in Front Plaid Pattern on 17 center sts, work in St st for 14 (17) sts.

Cont as established through pat row 16. Rep pat twice and through pat row 2—34 rows in total.

LEFT FRONT ARMHOLE AND NECK SHAPING

Work in pat until armhole row 14 (18).

Note: When working in pat, use Yarn C instead of Yarn B.

Work each armhole and each side of neck separately as follows:

Row 1 (RS row): Bind off 2 sts for armhole, k11 (14), work pat row 3 over next 7 sts, bind off 1 center st, leave rem 22 (25) sts for right front on a holder.

Row 2: Skp for neck, cont to work in pat, p to end.

Row 3: Bind off 2 sts for armhole, k9 (12), cont to work in pat.

Row 4: Cont to work in pat, p to end.

Row 5: Bind off 1 st for armhole, k8 (11), cont to work in pat.

Row 6: Skp for neck, cont to work in pat.

Row 7: K to beg of pat, work in pat.

Row 8: Rep row 4.

Row 9: K to beg of pat, work in pat.

Rows 10, 14, 18, 22, 26, (30): Rep row 6.

Rows 11, 13, 15, 17, 19, 21, 23, 25, 27, (29): Rep row 7.

Rows 12, 16, 20, 24, 28, (32): Rep row 4.

A total of 28 (32) rows have been worked.

Bind off rem 10 (12) sts for shoulders.

RIGHT FRONT ARMHOLE AND NECK SHAPING

Work to correspond to left front, reversing shaping.

Note: Beg with row 1 as WS row.

BACK

With Yarn B and straight needles, cast on 45 (51) sts.

Work in k3, p3 rib for 8 (10) rows.

Cut Yarn B.

Join Yarn A and work in St st for 16 rows.

BEG BACK PLAID PATTERN

Pat consists of 17 sts and 16 rows.

Join Yarn A and work 14 (17) sts in St st, work Back Plaid Pattern on 17 center sts, work in St st for 14 (17) sts.

Cont as established through pat row 16 twice and through pat row 2—34 rows in total.

ARMHOLE AND NECK SHAPING

Row 1 (RS row): Bind off 2 sts for armhole, k to end.

Row 2: Bind off 2 sts for armhole, p to end.

Rows 3-4: Rep rows 1 and 2 once more.

Row 5: Bind off 1 st for armhole, k to end.

Row 6: Bind off 1 st for armhole, p to end—35 (41) sts.

Rows 7-22 (7-26): Work in St st for 16 (20) more rows.

Row 23 (27): K14 (16) sts, bind off 7 (9) center sts for neck opening, k to end and leave rem 14 (16) sts for right back on a holder.

LEFT BACK SHOULDER AND NECK SHAPING

*Row 24 (28) (WS row): P all sts.

Row 25 (29): Bind off 2 sts, k to end.

Rows 26-27 (30-31): Rep from * twice—10 (12) sts.

Cont in St st until row 28 (32) has been completed.

Bind off all sts.

RIGHT BACK SHOULDER AND NECK SHAPING

Rows 24-28 (28-32): Work to correspond to left back shoulder and neck, reversing shaping.

FINISHING

Sew shoulder and side seams.

NECK BORDER

With RS facing, Yarn B, and circular needle, pick up and knit 25 (27) sts down left front slope, pick up and knit 1 center st, pick up and knit 25 (27) sts up right front slope and 21 (23) sts across back neck—72 (78) sts.

Note: Mark center st.

Rnd 1: Join and work in p1, k1 rib all around neck opening.

Rnd 2: Rib to 3 center sts, slip next 2 sts onto right needle, inserting needle from left to right into center st first, then into previous one, k next st, insert left needle from left to right, into 2 slipped sts and pass knit st through them, rib to end.

Rep rnd 1, 7 times.

Bind off loosely in rib pat.

ARMHOLE BORDER

With RS facing, Yarn B and circular needle, beg at side seam, pick up and knit 48 (52) sts around armhole opening.

Join and work in k1, p1 rib for 5 rnds.

Bind off loosely in rib pat.

STOPPED HERE

This project was knit with

For boys
(A) 2 balls of Lion Wool-Ease Chunky, 80% acrylic/20% wool yarn, bulky weight, 5oz/140g = approx 153yd/140m per ball, color #630-186

(B) 1 ball of Lion Wool-Ease Chunky, 80% acrylic/20% wool yarn, bulky weight, 5oz/140g = approx 153yd/140m per ball, color #630-152

(C) 1 ball of Lion Wool-Ease Chunky, 80% acrylic/20% wool yarn, bulky weight, 5oz/140g = approx 153yd/140m per ball, color #630-130

(D) 1 ball of Lion Wool-Ease Chunky, 80% acrylic/20% wool yarn, bulky weight, 5oz/140g = approx 153yd/140m per ball, color #630-133

For girls
(A) 2 balls of Lion Wool-Ease Chunky, 80% acrylic/20% wool yarn, bulky weight, 5oz/140g = approx 153yd/140m per ball, color #630-135

(B) 1 ball of Lion Wool-Ease Chunky, 80% acrylic/20% wool yarn, bulky weight, 5oz/140g = approx 153yd/140m per ball, color #630-140

(C) 1 ball of Lion Wool-Ease Chunky, 80% acrylic/20% wool yarn, bulky weight, 5oz/140g = approx 153yd/140m per ball, color #630-144

(D) 1 ball of Lion Wool-Ease Chunky, 80% acrylic/20% wool yarn, bulky weight, 5oz/140g = approx 153yd/140m per ball, color #630-186

Color and stitch key:

Yarn A ▓ : K on RS rows and P on WS rows
Yarn B ■ : K on RS rows and P on WS rows
Yarn C ▓ : K on RS rows and P on WS rows
Yarn D ▓ : K on RS rows and P on WS rows

Front Plaid Pattern

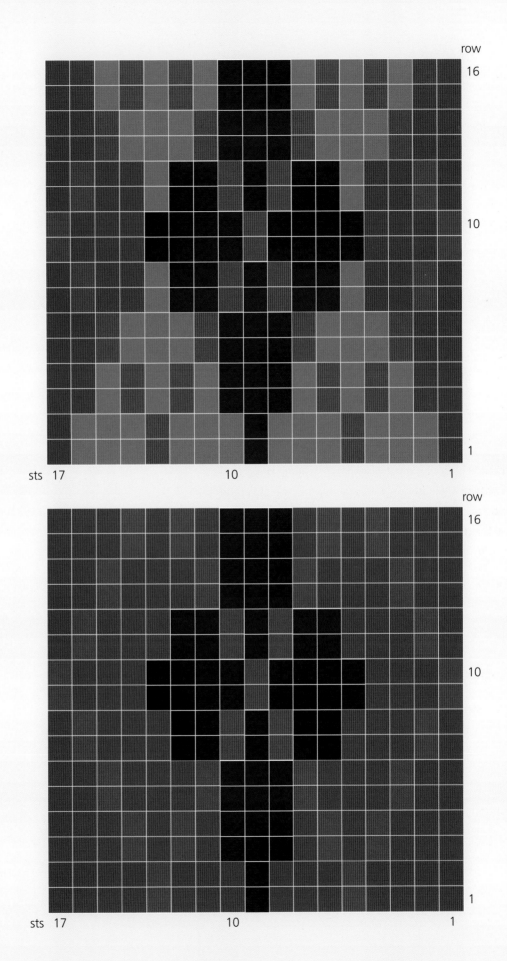

row
16

10

1

sts 17   10   1

Back Plaid Pattern

row
16

10

1

sts 17   10   1

The Fabled Cable Sweater

This beautiful cable knit sweater is as stylish as it is warm, and features a loose-fitting cowl neck and fashionable three-buttoned top.

EXPERIENCE LEVEL

■■■□ Intermediate

SIZES

Sized for 12–18 (24) months. Shown in size 24 months.

FINISHED MEASUREMENTS

Chest at underarm 22 (25)"/56 (63.5)cm

Length 12 (14)"/30.5 (35.5)cm

Upper arm (raglan) 10 (11)"/25.5 (28)cm

MATERIALS AND TOOLS

For boys

Yarn A (**SUPER BULKY 6**): 432yd/396m of Bulky weight yarn, acrylic/wool, in white with blue

For girls

Yarn B (**SUPER BULKY 6**): 432yd/396m of Bulky weight yarn, acrylic/wool, in red with bits of orange and blue

Size 10 (6mm) straight knitting needles OR SIZE TO OBTAIN GAUGE
Size 8 (5mm) circular knitting needle OR SIZE TO OBTAIN GAUGE

Cable needle

Stitch holder

Three ¾"/2cm buttons

Yarn needle

GAUGE

With larger size needles, in Rib and Cable pat, 18 sts and 28 rows to 5"/12.5cm

Measurements

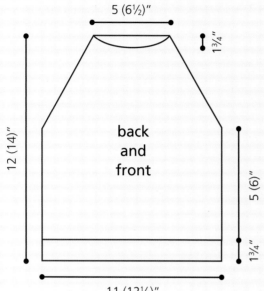

5 (6½)"

1¾"

back
and
front

12 (14)"

5 (6)"

1¾"

11 (12½)"

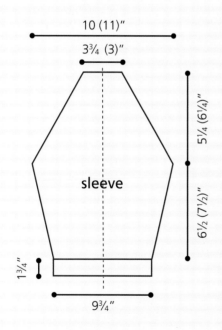

10 (11)"

3¾ (3)"

5¼ (6¼)"

sleeve

6½ (7½)"

1¾"

9¾"

Instructions

FRONT

With straight needles, cast on 45 (57) sts.

Work in k3, p3 rib for 12 rows.

BEG CABLE PATTERN

Pat consists of 21 sts.

Work in Cable pat for next 28 (34) rows as follows:

Note: For Cable pat, k the knits and p the purls on WS.

Rows 1–4: Beg at RS row, work 12 (18) sts in k3, p3 rib, work (k9, p3, k9) on 21 center sts, work in p3, k3 to end.

Note: C9B is equivalent to C6B, K next 3 sts. C9F is equivalent to K 3 sts, C6F. (See page 13 for cable pattern.)

Rows 5 and 17, (29) (cable twist): Work 12 (18) sts in k3, p3 rib, C9B (sl next 3 sts onto cable needle, move to back of work, k next 3 sts, k3 sts from cable needle, k next 3sts), p3, C9F (k3 sts, sl next 3 sts onto cable needle, move to front of work, k next 3 sts, k3 sts from cable needle), work in p3, k3 to end.

Rows 11 and 23 (cable twist): Work 12 (18) sts in k3, p3 rib, C9F, p3, C9B, work in p3, k3 to end.

Rows 6–10, 12–16, 18–22, 24–28, (30–34): Beg at WS row work 12 (18) sts in p3, k3 rib, work (p9, k3, p9) on 21 center sts, work in k3, p3 to end.

RAGLAN ARMHOLES SHAPING

Rows 1, 13 (cable twist): K2, k2tog, cont to rib until Cable pat begins, C9F, p3, C9B, rib across to last 4 sts, skp, k to end.

Rows 7, (19) (cable twist): K2, k2tog, cont to rib until Cable pat begins, C9B, p3, C9F, rib across to last 4 sts, skp, k to end.

Rows 2, 4, 6, 8, 10, 12, 14, 16, 18, (20, 22, 24): P3, rib until Cable pat begins, p9, k3, p9, rib across to last 3 sts, p3—27 (33) sts.

Rows 3, 5, 9, 11, 15, 17, (21, 23): K2, k2tog, cont to rib until Cable pat begins, k9, p3, k9, rib across to last 4 sts, skp, k to end—27 (33) sts rem.

NECK SHAPING

Row 1: K2, k2tog, k to last 17 (20) sts, bind off center 7 sts for neck, k to last 4 sts, skp, k to end and leave rem 9 (12) sts for left raglan armhole on a holder.

Work each raglan armhole and each side of neck separately.

RIGHT RAGLAN

Row 2 and all WS rows: P all sts.

Row 3, 5: Bind off 1 (2) sts for neck, k to last 4 sts, skp, k to end.

Row 7: Bind off 0 (1) sts for neck, k to last 4 sts, skp, k to end.

Row 9: Bind off rem sts.

LEFT RAGLAN

With WS facing, rejoin yarn to rem sts.

Row 2, 4: Bind off 1 (2) sts for neck, p to end.

Row 3, 5, 7: K2, k2tog, k to end.

Row 6: Bind off 0 (1) sts for neck, p to end.

Row 8: P all sts.

Bind off rem sts.

BACK

With straight needles, cast on 45 (57) sts.

Work in k3, p3 rib for 40 (46) rows.

RAGLAN ARMHOLES SHAPING

Row 1: K2, k2tog, rib to last 4 sts, skp, k to end.

Row 2: P3, rib to last 3 sts, p3.

Rep rows 1 and 2, 13 (16) times total—19 (25) sts.

Bind off rem 19 (25) sts.

SLEEVES

With straight needles, cast on 33 sts.

Work in k3, p3 rib for 12 rows.

BEG CABLE PATTERN

Pat consists of 9 sts.

Work in Cable pat for next 36 (42) rows and inc 1 st at each side of 3rd (first) row and every following 10th (8th) row 3 (5) times working increased sts in St st for a total of 39 (43) sts, as follows:

Rows 1–4: Work in k3, p3 rib until 9 center sts starts, k9, rib to end.

Rows 5, 17, 29, (41) (cable twist): Rib until 9 center sts starts, C9B, rib to end

Rows 11, 23, 35 (cable twist): Rib until 9 center sts starts, C9F, rib to end

Rows 6–10, 12–16, 18–22, 24–28, 30–34, 36, (37–40, 42): Beg at WS row, rib until 9 center sts starts, p9, rib to end.

There are now a total of 39 (43) sts.

RAGLAN SHAPING

Rows 1, 3, 7, 9, 13, 15,19, 21, 25, (27, 29, 31): K2, k2tog, cont to rib until Cable pat begins, k9, rib across to last 4 sts, skp, k to end.

Rows 2, 4, 6, 8, 10, 12, 14, 16, 18, 20, 22, 24, 26, (28, 30, 32): Rib until Cable pat begins, p9, rib across to end—13 (11) sts.

Rows 5, 17 (cable twist): K2, k2tog, cont to rib until Cable pat begins, C9B, rib across to last 4 sts, skp, k to end.

Rows 11, 23 (cable twist): K2, k2tog, cont to rib until Cable pat begins, C9F, rib across to last 4 sts, skp, k to end.

Bind off rem sts.

FINISHING

Sew side and sleeve seams.

Set in sleeves sewing through 2nd st from sleeve raglan edge to same sts of armhole raglan.

POLO NECK

With RS facing and circular needle, beginning 6 sts before right front raglan seam, pick up and k 66 (72) sts around neck opening as follows:

6 sts (insert needle under front leg of bind off sts) up right front neck to right raglan seam, 27 (30) sts across back neck to left raglan seam, 27 (30) sts down front neck to starting point and another 6 sts (insert needle under back leg of bind off sts) behind first 6 up right front neck to right raglan seam.

Row 1 (WS row): K6, work in k3, p3 rib to last 6 sts, k6.

Row 2: K6, work in p3, k3 rib to last 6 sts, k6.

Rows 3-5: Rep rows 1, 2 and 1.

Row 6 (Buttonhole and dec row): K2, bind off 2, k1, *(k3, p2tog, p1)—rep from * 9 (10) times, k6—57 (62) sts.

Row 7 (Buttonhole row): K6, work in k2, p3 rib to last 6 sts, k2, cast on 2, k2.

Rows 8–11, 14–16, (17, 20–22): K6, work in k3, p2 rib to last 6 sts, k6.

Rows 12 (18) (Buttonhole rows): K2, bind off 2, k1, work in k3, p2 rib to last 6 sts, k6.

Rows 13 (19) (Buttonhole rows): Work as for row 7.

Bind off all sts.

Sew on buttons.

This project was knit with

For boys
4 balls of Patons Shetland Chunky Tweeds, 75% acrylic/25% wool yarn, bulky weight, 3oz/85g = approx 108yd/99m, color #67024

For girls
4 balls of Patons Shetland Chunky Tweeds, 75% acrylic/25% wool yarn, bulky weight, 3oz/85g = approx 108yd/99m, color #67532

Baby's First Jumper

With lavender buttons and a delicate purse pocket, this pretty dress is feminine and fun. It's soft and comfortable too, letting little movers go anywhere they like.

EXPERIENCE LEVEL

■■□□ Easy

SIZES

Sized for 12 (18, 24) months. Shown in size 18 months.

FINISHED MEASUREMENTS

Waist 18 (19, 20)"/45.5 (48.5, 51)cm

Length from waist top to skirt bottom 11½ (12½, 14)"/ 29 (31.5, 35.5)cm

MATERIALS AND TOOLS

Yarn A 【4】: 356yd/326m of Medium weight yarn, cotton/acrylic, in pink

Yarn B 【4】: 178yd/163m of Medium weight yarn, cotton/acrylic, in light pink

Yarn C 【4】: 178yd/163m of Medium weight yarn, cotton/acrylic, in light purple

Size 6 (4mm) straight knitting needles OR SIZE TO OBTAIN GAUGE

Size D/3 (3mm) crochet hook

Four ¾"/2cm buttons

Yarn needle

GAUGE

With larger size needles, in Rib and Cable pat, 18 sts and 28 rows to 5"/12.5cm

Measurements

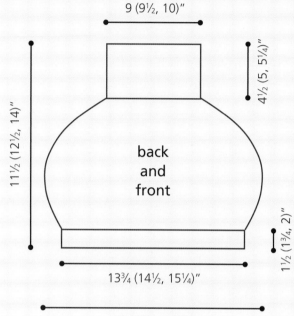

9 (9½, 10)"

4½ (5, 5¼)"

back and front

11½ (12½, 14)"

1½ (1¾, 2)"

13¾ (14½, 15¼)"

16 (17½, 18¾)"

Instructions

FRONT

Skirt

With Yarn B, cast on 78 (82, 86) sts.

Work in k2, p2 rib for 10 (10, 12) rows.

Cut Yarn B.

Join Yarn A and work in Garter st (k every row) for 8 (10, 12) rows, inc 1 st each side every 2nd row 4 (5, 6) times—86 (92, 98) sts.

Cont to work in Garter st for 10 (12, 16) more rows.

Work in Garter st for 40 (42, 44) rows, dec 1 st each side every 2nd row 20 (21, 22) times—46 (50, 54) sts.

Cut Yarn A.

Waist

Rows 1-24 (1-28, 1-30): Join Yarn B and work in k2, p2 rib for 24 (28, 30) rows.

Buttonhole rows

Row 25 (29, 31): (K2, p2) 3 times, bind off next 2 sts, p1, (k2, p2) across to last 14 sts, bind off next 2 sts, p1, (k2, p2) 2 times, k2.

Row 26 (30, 32): (P2, k2) 3 times, cast on 2 sts, k2, (p2, k2) across to last 12 sts, cast on next 2 sts, (k2, p2) 3 times.

Cont to work in k2, p2 rib for 5 more rows.

Bind off all sts in rib pat.

BACK

Skirt

Work as for front.

Waist

Rows 1-24 (1-28, 1-30): Work as for front until buttonhole rows.

BUTTONHOLE ROWS

Row 25 (29, 31): (K2, p2) 5 times, bind off next 2 sts, p1, k2, p2, bind off next 2 sts, p1, (k2, p2) 4 times, k2.

Row 26 (30, 32): (P2, k2) 5 times, cast on 2 sts, k2, p2, k2, cast on next 2 sts, (k2, p2) 5 times.

Cont to work in k2, p2 rib for 5 more rows.

Bind off all sts in rib pat.

STRAP

(Make 2)

With Yarn B, cast on 9 sts.

Work in Garter st for 110 (118, 128) rows.

Bind off all sts.

POCKET

Front

With Yarn C, cast on 17 sts.

Work in Garter st for 6 rows, inc 1 st each side every 2nd row 4 times.

Cont to work in Garter st for 4 more rows.

Work in Garter st for 6 rows, dec 1 st each side every 2nd row 4 times.

Cont to work in Garter st for 4 more rows.

Bind off all sts.

Back

Work as for front.

Ribbon

With Yarn A and hook, ch 60 sts. Cut yarn and tie ends.

Sew pocket's bottom and side seams.

Insert ribbon into 4th row from top at front middle of pocket. Draw ribbon around and pull out at front middle of pocket. Knot each side of ribbon.

FINISHING

Sew side seams.

Sew buttons to each end of each strap.

Cross straps in back to button.

Attach pocket about 28 rows above ribbing, and about 30 sts to the left of right edge. Sew pocket on through back middle of pocket, about 6 rows from the top, to corresponding sts in jumper.

This project was knit with

(A) 2 balls of TLC Cotton Plus, 51% cotton/49% acrylic yarn, medium weight, 3oz/100g = approx 178yd/163m per ball, color #3707

(B) 1 ball of TLC Cotton Plus, 51% cotton/49% acrylic yarn, medium weight, 3oz/100g = approx 178yd/163m per ball, color #3706

(C) 1 ball of TLC Cotton Plus, 51% cotton/49% acrylic yarn, medium weight, 3oz/100g = approx 178yd/163m per ball, color #3590

Kimono

With a simple tie at the top and a wide bottom, this sweater is comfy to wear, and easy to put on. As for the pattern, what vegetable could be friendlier than the familiar carrot!

EXPERIENCE LEVEL

■■■☐ Intermediate

SIZES

Sized for newborn–3 months (6, 12, 18 months). Shown in size newborn–3 months.

FINISHED MEASUREMENTS

Chest (closed) 21 (23, 25, 27)"/53.5 (58.5, 63.5, 68.5)cm

Length 8 (9 1/2, 11, 12 1/2)"/20.5 (24, 28, 31.5)cm

Upper arm 8 (9, 10, 11)"/20.5 (23, 25.5, 28)cm

MATERIALS AND TOOLS

Yarn A 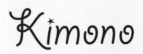 : 207yd/188m of Medium weight yarn, cotton/acrylic, in light green

Yarn B 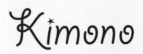 : 207yd/188m of Medium weight yarn, cotton/acrylic, in yellow

Yarn C 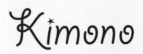 : 207yd/188m of Medium weight yarn, cotton/acrylic, in burnt orange

Size 4 (3.5mm) straight knitting needles OR SIZE TO OBTAIN GAUGE

Size D/3 (3mm) crochet hook

Four ¾"/2cm buttons

Stitch holder

Two-part sewable ¼"/7mm snap

Yarn needle

GAUGE

In St st, 20 sts and 30 rows to 4"/10cm

Measurements

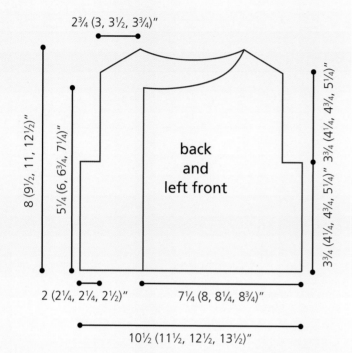

2¾ (3, 3½, 3¾)"

8 (9½, 11, 12½)"

5¼ (6, 6¾, 7¼)"

3¾ (4¼, 4¾, 5¼)" 3¾ (4¼, 4¾, 5¼)"

back
and
left front

2 (2¼, 2¼, 2½)"

7¼ (8, 8¼, 8¾)"

10½ (11½, 12½, 13½)"

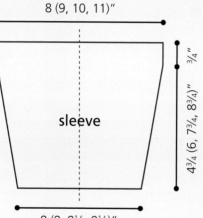

8 (9, 10, 11)"

¾"

4¾ (6, 7¾, 8¾)"

sleeve

8 (8, 8¼, 8¼)"

Instructions

BACK

With Yarn A, cast on 54 (58, 64, 68) sts.

Work in St st for 28 (32, 36, 40) rows.

ARMHOLE SHAPING

Row 1: Bind off 5 (6, 6, 7) sts, k to end.

Row 2: Bind off 5 (6, 6, 7) sts, p to end.

Cont to work in St st for 26 (30, 34, 38) more rows.

SHOULDERS AND BACK NECK SHAPING

Row 1 (RS): Bind off 5 (6, 6, 7) sts for right shoulder, k15 (16, 18, 18), bind off center 12 (12, 14, 16) sts for neck, k to end.

Work each shoulder and each side of neck separately.

Leave rem 16 (17, 19, 19) sts for right shoulder on a holder.

LEFT SHOULDER

Row 2 (WS): Bind off 5 (6, 6, 7) sts for shoulder, p to end.

Row 3: Bind off 3 sts for neck, k to end.

Row 4: Bind off 3 (4, 5, 5) sts for shoulder, p to end.

Row 5: Bind off 2 sts for neck, k to end.

Row 6: Bind off 5 (5, 6, 6) sts for shoulder, p to end.

Row 7: Bind off last 3 sts for neck.

RIGHT SHOULDER

With WS facing, rejoin yarn to rem 16 (17, 19, 19) sts.

Row 2 (WS): Bind off 3 sts for neck, p to end.

Row 3: Bind off 3 (4, 5, 5) sts for shoulder, k to end.

Row 4: Bind off 2 sts for neck, p to end.

Row 5: Bind off 5 (5, 6, 6) sts for shoulder, k to end.

Row 6: Bind off last 3 sts for neck.

LEFT FRONT

With Yarn A, cast on 36 (40, 42, 44) sts.

Work in St st for 28 (32, 36, 40) rows.

ARMHOLE SHAPING

Row 1: Bind off 5 (6, 6, 7) sts, k to end—31 (34, 36, 37) sts.

Cont to work in St st for 21 (25, 29, 33) more rows.

LEFT SHOULDER AND FRONT NECK SHAPING

Row 1 (WS row): Bind off 9 sts for neck, p to end—22 (25, 27, 28) sts.

Row 2: K all sts.

Row 3: Bind off 4 (5, 5, 5) sts for neck, p to end.

Row 4: K all sts.

Row 5: Bind off 3 (4, 4, 4) sts for neck, p to end.

Row 6: K all sts.

Row 7: Bind off 3 sts for neck, p to end.

Row 8: Bind off 5 (5, 6, 6) sts for shoulder, k to end.

Row 9: Bind off 2 (2, 2, 3) sts for neck, p to end.

Row 10: Bind off 3 (4, 5, 5) sts for shoulder, k to end.

Row 11: Bind off rem 2 sts for neck.

RIGHT FRONT

With Yarn B, cast on 36 (40, 42, 44) sts.

Work in St st for 4 (8, 12, 16) rows.

BEG CARROT PATTERN

Pat consists of 22 sts and 40 rows.

Work 7 (9, 10, 11) sts in St st, work in Carrot Pattern on 22 center sts, work 7 (9, 10, 11) sts in St st.

Cont as established through pat row 23.

ARMHOLE SHAPING

Row 1 (WS row): Bind off 5 (6, 6, 7) sts, p1 (2, 3, 3), work pat row 24 over next 22 sts, p to end—31 (34, 36, 37) sts.

Row 2: K7 (9, 10, 11) sts, cont to work in pat on 22 center sts, k to end.

Row 3: P2 (3, 4, 4) sts, work in Carrot Pattern on 22 center sts, p to end.

Rep rows 2 and 3 through end of pat.

Work in St st for 4 (8, 12, 16) more rows.

RIGHT SHOULDER AND FRONT NECK SHAPING

Row 1 (RS row): Bind off 9 sts for neck, k to end.

Row 2: P all sts.

Row 3: Bind off 4 (5, 5, 5) sts for neck, k to end.

Row 4: P all sts.

Row 5: Bind off 3 (4, 4, 4) sts for neck, k to end.

Row 6: P all sts.

Row 7: Bind off 3 sts for neck, k to end.

Row 8: Bind off 5(5, 6, 6) sts for shoulder, p to end.

Row 9: Bind off 2 (2, 2, 3) sts for neck, k to end.

Row 10: Bind off 3 (4, 5, 5) sts for shoulder, p to end.

Row 11: Bind off rem 2 sts for neck.

SLEEVES

Left sleeve

With Yarn B, cast on 40 (40, 42, 42) sts.

Work in St st for 4 (4, 8, 10) rows.

BEG LEFT SLEEVE PATTERN

Pat consists of 8 sts and 4 rows.

Work 0 (0, 1, 1) st in St st, *work in Left Sleeve Pattern on 8 sts, rep from * 5 times, work 0 (0, 1, 1) st in St st to end.

Cont as established for 4 rows.

Work in St st, inc 0 (1, 1, 1) st at each side of next and every following 8th (14th, 12th, 8th) row 4 (3, 4, 7) times in all—40 (46, 50, 56) sts.

Cont to work in St st for 7 more rows. End with WS row.

Bind off all sts.

RIGHT SLEEVE

Work as for left sleeve and following Right Sleeve Pattern instead of Left Sleeve Pattern, using Yarn C.

FINISHING

Sew shoulder seams.

Set in sleeves, sewing top of sleeve along armhole edge and sides of sleeve (last 7 rows) to armhole bound-off edges. Sew side and sleeve seams. Sew one part of snap onto RS of top edge of left front. Close kimono and mark corresponding place on WS of right front. Sew other part of snap onto marked place on WS of right front.

CROCHETED EDGING

With RS facing and Yarn A, insert hook in bottom corner of left front.

Ch 3, sk, sl st in next cast on st of Kimono bottom, *ch 2, sk, sl st next cast on st. Rep from * across to bottom corner of right front, cont along front edge up to top right front corner (inserting hook under edge sts), across neck opening (inserting hook into Bind off sts) to top left front corner and along left front edge down to bottom left front corner. Join and fasten off.

Work same for sleeve edgings.

RIBBONS

With RS facing and Yarn A, insert hook in top corner of right front, sl st, ch 40. Cut yarn and tie ends. Close kimono and mark corresponding place on RS of left front. With Yarn C, insert hook through marked place on left front, sl st, ch 40. Cut yarn and tie ends.

This project was knit with

(A) 1 ball of Lion Cotton Ease, 50% cotton/50% acrylic yarn, medium weight, 3½oz/100g = approx 207yd/188m per ball, color #830-194

(B) 1 ball of Lion Cotton Ease, 50% cotton/50% acrylic yarn, medium weight, 3½oz/100g = approx 207yd/188m per ball, color #830-186

(C) 1 ball of Lion Cotton Ease, 50% cotton/50% acrylic yarn, medium weight, 3½oz/100g = approx 207yd/188m per ball, color #830-134

Carrot Pattern

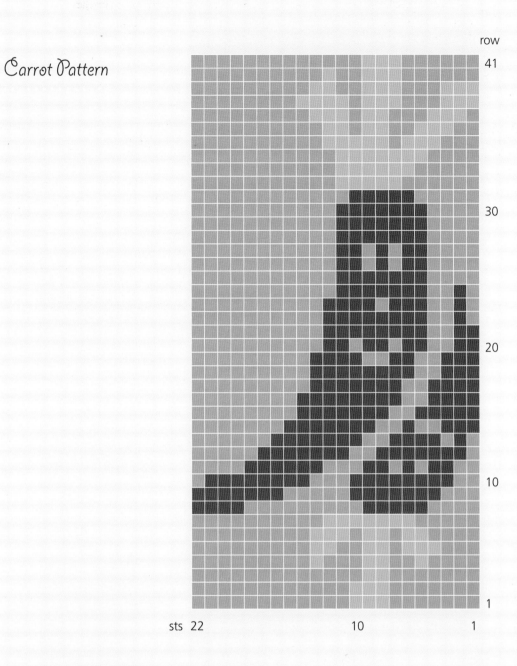

row

41

30

20

10

1

sts 22   10   1

Left Sleeve Pattern

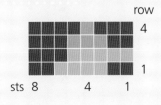

row

4

1

sts 8   4   1

Right Sleeve Pattern

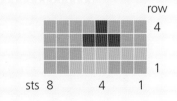

row

4

1

sts 8   4   1

Color and stitch key:

Yarn A   : K on RS rows and P on WS rows

Yarn B   : K on RS rows and P on WS rows

Yarn C   : K on RS rows and P on WS rows

Summer Overalls

These wide-legged, Capri-style overalls are loose and comfortable. Stylish and cute, they are excellent for toddlers who like to move.

EXPERIENCE LEVEL

■■■ ▭ Intermediate

SIZES

Sized for 12 (18, 24) months. Shown in size 18 months.

FINISHED MEASUREMENTS

Waist 16½ (18, 18½)"/42 (45.5, 47)cm

Length from waist top to legs bottom 12 (13, 14)"/30.5 (33, 35.5)cm

MATERIALS AND TOOLS

Yarn A **MEDIUM 4** : 356yd/326m of Medium weight yarn, cotton/acrylic, in variegated blue and green

Yarn B **MEDIUM 4** : 178yd/163m of Medium weight yarn, cotton/acrylic, in light green

Sizes 6 (4mm) and 8 (5mm) straight knitting needles OR SIZE TO OBTAIN GAUGE

Stitch holder

Four ¾"/2cm buttons

Yarn needle

GAUGE

With larger size needles, in Garter st, 19 sts and 34 rows to 4"/10cm

With smaller size needles, in Rib pat, 24 sts and 34 rows to 4"/10cm

Measurements

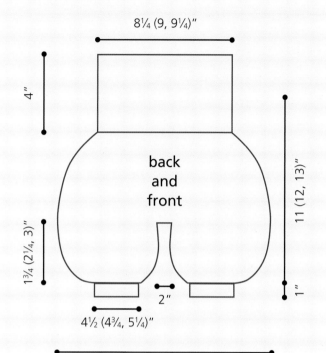

8¼ (9, 9¼)"

4"

back
and
front

11 (12, 13)"

1¾ (2¼, 3)"

2"

1"

4½ (4¾, 5¼)"

20 (22, 24)"

Instructions

BACK

Left leg

With Yarn B and smaller needles, cast on 27 (29, 31) sts.

Work in k1, p1 rib for 8 rows.

With larger needles, k one row across.

K next row, inc each 2nd st 13 (14, 15) times—40 (43, 46) sts. Cut Yarn B.

Join Yarn A.

Work in Garter st as following: (2 rows Yarn B, 2 rows Yarn A) 1 (2, 2) times, inc 1 st each side every 2nd row 2 (4, 4) times—44 (51, 54) sts.

Cont to work in Garter st for 10 (8, 14) more rows, change yarn every 3rd row.

Place sts on a holder.

RIGHT LEG

Work as for left leg. Don't place on a holder.

LEG JOINING

Next row (RS): With Yarn A, k across sts of right leg, cast on 10 sts, k across sts of left leg from holder—98 (112, 118) sts.

K one more row.

Join Yarn B.

Work in Garter st as follows: (2 rows Yarn B, 2 rows Yarn A) 3 times, dec 1 st each side every 2nd row 6 times—86 (100, 106) sts.

Cut Yarn B.

With Yarn A cont to work in Garter st for 36 (46, 48) rows, dec 1 st each side every 2nd row 18 (23, 24) times—50 (54, 58) sts.

WAIST

Rows 1-22: Join Yarn A and smaller needles work in k2, p2 rib for 22 rows.

Buttonhole rows

Row 23: (K2, p2) 5 times, bind off next 2 sts, p1, (k2, p2) 1 (2, 3) times, bind off next 2 sts, p1, (k2, p2) 4 times, k2.

Row 24: (P2, k2) 5 times, cast on 2 sts, k2, (p2, k2) 1 (2, 3) times, cast on next 2 sts, (k2, p2) 5 times.

Rows 25-29: Cont to work in k2, p2 rib for 5 more rows.

Bind off all sts in rib pat.

FRONT

Right leg

Work to correspond to back left leg.

LEFT LEG

Work to correspond to back right leg.

LEG JOINING

Next row (RS) With Yarn A, k across sts of left leg, cast on 10 sts, k across sts of right leg from holder—98 (112, 118) sts.

Cont to work same as for back.

WAIST

Rows 1-22: Work as for back until buttonhole rows.

Buttonhole rows

Row 23: (K2, p2) 3 times, bind off next 2 sts, p1, (k2, p2) across to last 14 sts, bind off next 2 sts, p1, (k2, p2) 2 times, k2.

Row 24: (P2, k2) 3 times, cast on 2 sts, k2, (p2, k2) across to last 12 sts, cast on next 2 sts, (k2, p2) 3 times.

Rows 25-29: Cont to work in k2, p2 rib for 5 more rows.

Bind off all sts in rib pat.

STRAP

(Make 2)

With Yarn B and smaller needles, cast on 9 sts.

Work in Garter st for 110 (118, 128) rows.

Bind off all sts.

FINISHING

Sew inside leg and side seams.

Sew buttons to each end of each strap.

Cross straps in back to button.

This project was knit with

(A) 2 balls of TLC Cotton Plus, 51% cotton/49% acrylic yarn, medium weight, 3½oz/100g = approx 178yd/163m per ball, color #3324

(B) 1 ball of TLC Cotton Plus, 51% cotton/49% acrylic yarn, medium weight, 3½oz/100g = approx 178yd/163m per ball, color #3645

Springtime Cardigan

With gentle shades of yellow, sky blue, and green, this cardigan is as bright as the first spring sunshine, and perfect for wearing when weather starts to warm up.

EXPERIENCE LEVEL

◼◼◼☐ Intermediate

SIZES

Sized for newborn–3 months (6–12, 18–24) months. Shown in size newborn–3 months.

FINISHED MEASUREMENTS

Chest (buttoned) 18 (22, 26)"/45.5 (56, 66)cm

Length 10¾ (12¼, 13¾)"/27.5 (31, 35)cm

Upper arm 9½ (10½, 11)"/24 (26.5, 28)cm

MATERIALS AND TOOLS

Yarn A **MEDIUM (4)**: 342yd/312m of Medium weight yarn, cotton, in yellow

Yarn B **MEDIUM (4)**: 150yd/137m of Medium weight yarn, cotton, in blue, green, yellow and white

Yarn C **MEDIUM (4)**: 171yd/156m of Medium weight yarn, cotton/acrylic, in light green

Size 8 (5 mm) straight knitting needles OR SIZE TO OBTAIN GAUGE

Size E/4 (3.5mm) crochet hook

Stitch holder

Three ⅜"/1cm buttons

Yarn needle

GAUGE

In pat, 20 sts and 20 rows to 4"/10cm

Measurements

SPRINGTIME PATTERN

Pat consists of 10 sts and 2 rows.

Row 1: K1, YO, k3, slip1, k2tog, PSSO, k3, YO.

Row 2 and all WS rows: P across.

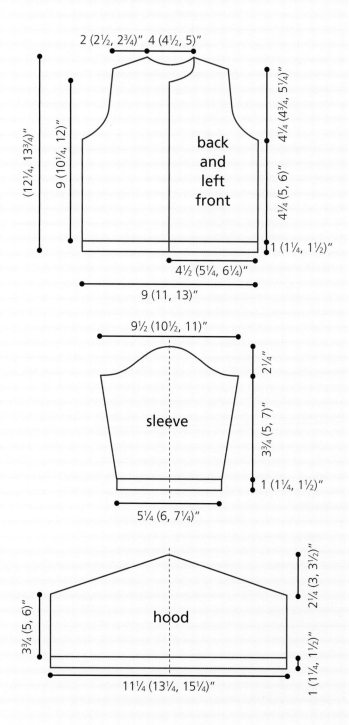

Instructions

BACK

With Yarn B, cast on 45 (55, 65) sts.

Work in Garter st for 6 (8, 10) rows. Cut Yarn B.

BEG SPRINGTIME PATTERN

Join Yarn A.

*Row 1 (RS): K2, work row 1 of pat 4 (5, 6) times, k to end.

Row 2: P across.

Rep from * 11 (13, 15) times in all.

ARMHOLE SHAPING

Row 1: Bind off 2, k3, YO, * slip1, k2tog, PSSO, k3, YO, k1, YO, k3— rep from * 3 (4, 5) times, slip1, k2tog, PSSO, YO, k to end.

Row 2: Bind off 2, p across.

Row 3: Bind off 1, k2, YO, *slip1, k2tog, PSSO, k3, YO, k1, YO, k3—rep from * 3 (4, 5) times, slip1, k2tog, PSSO, YO, k to end.

Row 4: Bind off 1, p across—39 (49, 59) sts.

*Row 5: K3, YO, *slip1, k2tog, PSSO, k3, YO, k1, YO, k3—rep from * 3 (4, 5) times, slip1, k2tog, PSSO, YO, k to end.

Row 6: P across.

Rep from * 11 (13, 15) times in all.

BACK NECK AND SHOULDERS SHAPING

Row 1 (RS): Bind off 5 (7, 9) for right shoulder, k7 (9, 13), bind off center 13 (15, 17) sts for neck, k to end.

Work each side of neck and shoulder separately.

Place rem 8 (10, 14) sts for right shoulder on a holder.

LEFT SHOULDER

Row 2 (WS): Bind off 5 (7, 9) for shoulder, p to end.

Row 3: K across.

Row 4: Bind off 4 (6, 8) for shoulder, p to end.

Row 5: Bind off rem sts.

RIGHT SHOULDER

Row 2 (WS): Purl.

Row 3 (RS): Bind off 4 (6, 8) for shoulder, k to end.

Row 4: Bind off rem sts.

RIGHT FRONT

With Yarn B, cast on 22 (27, 32) sts.

Work in Garter st for 6 (8, 10) rows.

BEG SPRINGTIME PATTERN

Note: When changing colors, twist yarns tog on WS to prevent holes.

*Row 1 (RS): With Yarn B, k6 for border, with Yarn A, k1 (5, 1), work row 1 of pat 1 (1, 2) times, k to end.

Row 2: With Yarn A, p to last 6 sts, with Yarn B, k to end.

Rep from * 11 (13, 15) times in all.

ARMHOLE SHAPING

Row 1: With Yarn B, k6 for border, with Yarn A, k1 (5, 1), work row 1 of pat 1 (1, 2) times, k5 (6, 5).

Row 2: With Yarn A, bind off 2, p to last 6 sts, with Yarn B, k6.

Row 3: With Yarn B, k6 for border, with Yarn A, k1 (5, 1), work row 1 of pat 1 (1, 2) times, k3 (4, 3).

Row 4: With Yarn A, bind off 1, p to last 6 sts, with Yarn B, k6.

*Row 5: With Yarn B, k6 for border, with Yarn A, k1 (5, 1), work row 1 of pat 1 (1, 2) times, k2 (3, 2).

Row 6: With Yarn A, p to last 6 sts, with Yarn B, k6.

Rep from * 9 (11, 13) times.

FRONT NECK AND SHOULDERS SHAPING

Row 1 (RS): With Yarn B, bind off 3 for neck, k2, with Yarn A, k1 (5, 1), work row 1 of pat 1 (1, 2) times, k to end.

Row 2: With Yarn A, p to last 3 sts, with Yarn B, k to end.

Row 3: With Yarn B, bind off 2 for neck, with Yarn A, k1 (5, 1), work row 1 of pat 1 (1, 2) times, k to end. Cut Yarn B.

Row 4: With Yarn A, p across.

Row 5: Bind off 1 (2, 2) for neck, k to end.

Row 6: Bind off 5 (7, 9) for shoulder, p to end.

Row 7: Bind off 1 (1, 2) for neck, k to end.

Row 8: Bind off 4 (6, 8) for shoulder, p to end.

Bind off rem sts.

LEFT FRONT

Work to correspond to left side, reversing armhole, front neck and shoulders shaping.

SLEEVES

With Yarn B, cast on 27 (31, 37) sts.

Work in Garter st for 6 (8, 10) rows.

BEG SPRINGTIME PATTERN

Join Yarn A.

Row 1 (RS): K3 (5, 3), work row 1 of pat 2 (2, 3) times, k to end.

Row 2 and each WS row: P across.

Rows 3-4 (3-6, 3-8): Rep rows 1 and 2—1 (2, 3) more times.

Row 5 (7, 9): K2, inc 1, k0 (2, 0), work row 1 of pat 2 (2, 3) times, k to last 3 sts, inc 1, k2.

Row 7 (9, 11): K4 (6, 4), work row 1 of pat 2 (2, 3) times, k to end.

Row 9-10 (11-14, 13-18): Rep rows 7 and 2—1 (2, 3) more times.

Row 11 (15, 19): K2, inc 1, k1 (3, 1), work row 1 of pat 2 (2, 3) times, k to last 3 sts, inc 1, k2.

Row 13 (17, 21): K5 (7, 5), work row 1 of pat 2 (2, 3) times, k to end.

Row 15-16 (19-22, 23-28): Rep rows 13 and 2—1 (2, 3) more times.

Row 17 (23, 29): K2, inc 1, k2 (4, 2), work row 1 of pat 2 (2, 3) times, k to last 3 sts, inc 1, k2.

Row 19 (25, 31): K6 (8, 6), work row 1 of pat 2 (2, 3) times, k to end—33 (37, 43) sts.

Row 20 (26, 32): P across.

SLEEVE TOP SHAPING

Row 1: Bind off 3, k2 (4, 2), work row 1 of pat 2 (2, 3) times, k to end.

Row 2: Bind off 3, p to end.

Row 3: Bind off 2, k0 (2, 0), work row 1 of pat 2 (2, 3) times, k to end.

Row 4: Bind off 2, p to end.

FOR NEWBORN–3 MONTHS SIZE ONLY

Row 5: Bind off 1, k1, YO, k2, slip1, k2tog, PSSO, k3, YO, k1, YO, k3, slip1, k2tog, PSSO, k2, YO, k to end.

Row 6: Bind off 1, p to end.

Row 7: Bind off 1, k1, YO, k1, slip1, k2tog, PSSO, k3, YO, k1, YO, k3, slip1, k2tog, PSSO, k1, YO, k to end.

Row 8: Bind off 1, p to end.

Row 9: Bind off 2, k1, k2tog, k3, YO, k1, YO, k3, k2tog, k to end.

FOR 6–12 MONTHS SIZE ONLY

Row 5: Bind off 1, k1, work row 1 of pat 2 times, k to end.

Row 6: Bind off 1, p to end.

Row 7: Bind off 1, work row 1 of pat 2 times, k to end.

Row 8: Bind off 1, p to end.

Row 9: Bind off 1, k1, YO, k1, slip1, k2tog, PSSO, k3, YO, k1, YO, k3, slip1, k2tog, PSSO, k1, YO, k to end.

FOR 18–24 MONTHS SIZE ONLY

Row 5: Bind off 1, k1, YO, k2, slip1, k2tog, PSSO, k3, YO, work row 1 of pat 1 time, k1, YO, k3, slip1, k2tog, PSSO, k2, YO, k to end.

Row 6: Bind off 1, p to end.

Row 7: Bind off 1, k1, YO, k1, slip1, k2tog, PSSO, k3, YO, work row 1 of pat 1 time, k1, YO, k3, slip1, k2tog, PSSO, k1, YO, k to end.

Row 8: Bind off 1, p to end.

Row 9: Bind off 2, k1, k2tog, k3, YO, work row 1 of pat 1 time, k1, YO, k3, k2tog, k to end.

FOR ALL SIZES

Row 10: Bind off 2, p to end.

Row 11: Bind off 3, k to end.

Row 12: Bind off 3, p to end.

Bind off all sts.

HOOD

With Yarn B, cast on 57 (67, 77) sts.

Work in Garter st for 6 (8, 10) rows.

BEG PAT

Join Yarn A.

Row 1 (RS): K3, work row 1 of pat 5 (6, 7) times, k to end.

Row 2: P across.

Rows 3-18 (3-24, 3-30): Rep rows 1 and 2—8 (11, 14) more times.

Row 19 (25, 31): Bind off 5, k2, k2tog, k3, YO, work row 1 of pat 3 (4, 5) times, k1, YO, k3, k2tog, k to end.

Row 20 (26, 32): Bind off 5, p to end.

Row 21 (27, 33): Bind off 5, k2, work row 1 of pat 3 (4, 5) times, k to end.

Row 22 (28, 34): Bind off 5, p to end—37 (47, 57) sts.

Row 23 (29, 35): Bind off 4, k3, k2tog, k3, YO, work row 1 of pat 2 (3, 4) times k1, YO, k3, k2tog, k to end.

Row 24 (30, 36): Bind off 4, p to end—29 (39, 49) sts.

Row 25 (31, 37): Bind off 4, k4, work row 1 of pat 1 (2, 3) times, k to end.

Row 26 (32, 38): Bind off 4, p to end—21 (31, 41) sts.

Row 27 (33, 39): Bind off 4, work row 1 of pat 1 (2, 3) times, k to end.

Row 28 (34, 40): Bind off 4, p to end—13 (23, 33) sts.

FOR 6–12 (18–24) MONTHS SIZE ONLY

Row 35 (41): Bind off 4, k1, work row 1 of pat 1 (2) time, k to end.

Row 36 (42): Bind off 4, p to end—15 (25) sts.

FOR 18–24 MONTHS SIZE ONLY

Row 43: Bind off 4, k2, work row 1 of pat 1 time, k to end.

Row 44: Bind off 4, p to end—17 sts.

FOR ALL SIZES

Next row 1: Bind off 4, k to end.

Next row 2: Bind off 4, p to end.

Bind off all sts.

FINISHING

Sew shoulder seams. Sew side and sleeve seams. Set in sleeves sewing last ¼"/6mm at top of sleeve to bound-off armhole sts. Sew hood back seam. With WS of hood and cardigan facing, attach hood to neck opening, sewing it on 3 sts from top left edge all around neck opening to 3 sts from top right edge.

CROCHETED EDGING

With RS facing and Yarn C, insert hook in bottom corner of left front.

Ch 1, sc 2 into corner, sc 1 into each cast on st along cardigan bottom, sc 3 into bottom right front corner, sc 1 evenly along right front edge up to top right front corner, inserting hook under edge sts, sc 3 into corner, sc 1 across each border and hood opening, sc 3 into top left corner. Sc 1 under edge sts along left front edge down to bottom left front corner, making 3 button loops spaced evenly along. Join and fasten off.

Work sc 1 across sleeve edgings. Join and fasten off.

BUTTON LOOPS

Ch 5, sc 1 into next st.

Sew on buttons.

This project was knit with

(A) 2 balls of Bernat Cottontots, 100% cotton yarn, medium weight, 3½oz/100g = approx 171yd/156m per ball, color #90616

(B) 1 ball of Bernat Cottontots, 100% cotton yarn, medium weight, 3½oz/100g = approx 171yd/156m per ball, color #91713

(C) 1 ball of Lion Cotton Ease, 100% cotton yarn, medium weight, 3½oz/100g = approx 171yd/156m color #830-194

Hat with Earflaps

Playful yet practical, this hat features a fluffy visor and top, ear flaps and a pompon. It's a fun, functional design youngsters will be happy to have on their heads!

EXPERIENCE LEVEL

■■■□ Intermediate

SIZES

Sized for 12 (18, 24) months. Shown in size 24 months.

FINISHED MEASUREMENTS

Head circumference 17 (18, 19)"/43 (45.5, 48.5)cm

MATERIALS AND TOOLS

Yarn A **SUPER BULKY 6** : 153yd/140m of Bulky weight yarn, acrylic/wool, in orange

Yarn B **SUPER BULKY 6** : 60yd/54m of Bulky weight yarn, polyester, in light green

Yarn C **SUPER BULKY 6** : 153yd/140m of Bulky weight yarn, acrylic/wool, in green

Size 10 (6mm) straight knitting needles OR SIZE TO OBTAIN GAUGE

Size H/8 (5mm) crochet hook

Two stitch holders

Tracing paper, pencil, and permanent marker

Scissors

Large piece of cardboard

Yarn needle

GAUGE

In St st, 14 sts and 19 rows to 4"/10cm

Instructions

EAR FLAPS

(Make 2)

With Yarn A, CO 5 sts.

Work in St st for 2 rows.

Cont to work in St st, inc 1 st at each side after first and before last st of next and every following 2nd row 4 (5, 5) times—13 (15, 15) sts. End with WS row.

Cont to work in St st for 6 (8, 10) rows more.

Place all sts onto holder.

VISOR

With 2 strands of Yarn B, CO 9 (9, 11) sts.

Work in St st for 2 rows.

Cont to work in St st, inc 1 st at each side after first and before last st of next and every following 2nd row 3 times—15 (15, 17) sts. End with WS row.

Place all sts onto holder.

HAT

With Yarn A, CO 9 (9, 10) sts, place 13 (15, 15) sts of first ear flap from holder back onto needle, place 15 (15, 17) sts of visor from holder back onto needle, place 13 (15, 15) sts of 2nd ear flap from holder back onto needle, CO 9 (9, 10) sts—59 (63, 67) sts.

Work on all sts in St st for 16 (18, 18) rows.

HAT TOP SHAPING

Row 1: K11 (12, 13), k2tog, k1, skp, k27 (29, 31), k2tog, k1, skp, k11 (12, 13)—55 (59, 63) sts.

Row 2 and each WS row: P across.

Join 2 strands of Yarn B.

Row 3: K10 (11, 12), k2tog, k1, skp, k25 (27, 29), k2tog, k1, skp, k10 (11, 12)—51 (55, 59) sts.

With Yarn A,

Row 5: K9 (10, 11), k2tog, k1, skp, k23 (25, 27), k2tog, k1, skp, k9 (10, 11)—47 (51, 55) sts.

With 2 strands of Yarn B,

Row 7: K8 (9, 10), k2tog, k1, skp, k21 (23, 25), k2tog, k1, skp, k8 (9, 10)—43 (47, 51) sts.

With Yarn A,

Row 9: K7 (8, 9), k2tog, k1, skp, k19 (21, 23), k2tog, k1, skp, k7 (8, 9)—39 (43, 47) sts.

With 2 strands of Yarn B,

Row 11: K6 (7, 8), k2tog, k1, skp, k17 (19, 21), k2tog, k1, skp, k6 (7, 8)—35 (39, 43) sts.

With Yarn A,

Row 13: K5 (6, 7), k2tog, k1, skp, k15 (17, 19), k2tog, k1, skp, k5 (6, 7)—31 (35, 39) sts. Cut Yarn A.

With 2 strands of Yarn B,

FOR 12 MONTHS SIZE ONLY

Row 15: K2tog 7 times, slip 1, k2tog, PSSO, k2tog 7 times—15 sts.

Row 17: BO all sts.

FOR 18 MONTHS SIZE ONLY

Row 15: K5, k2tog, k1, skp, k15, k2tog, k1, skp, k5—31 sts.

Row 17: K2tog 7 times, slip 1, k2tog, PSSO, k2tog 7 times—15 sts.

Row 19: BO all sts.

FOR 24 MONTHS SIZE ONLY

Row 15: K6, k2tog, k1, skp, k17, k2tog, k1, skp, k6—35 sts.

Row 17: K5, k2tog, k1, skp, k15, k2tog, k1, skp, k5—31 sts.

Row 19: K2tog 7 times, slip 1, k2tog, PSSO, k2tog 7 times—15 sts.

Row 21: BO all sts.

Cut yarn, leaving a 10"/25cm tail.

Thread needle with tail and *insert through all sts, from first to last.

Draw yarn back through all sts and tighten. Rep from * twice.

Cut yarn, tie ends, and hide tails.

POMPON

Make 1 using Yarn C (see Pompon Template 1, page 127, and see Pompon page 12).

Sew pompon onto hat top.

FINISHING

Crocheted edging

With RS and one ear facing, top close to you and Yarn C, insert hook into bottom corner of ear, ch 1, sc 2 into same corner, sc 1 evenly all around hat bottom, along first ear down to hat back, along back to 2nd ear, up to ear bottom corner, sc 3 into the corner, down to visor, across visor, and up to first ear bottom corner. End with sl st and fasten off.

SIDE STRAPS

Insert hook into each ear bottom corner, fold Yarn C in half, pull yarn through, and with 2 strands, ch 30. Cut yarn and tie ends.

FRONT STRAP

With 3 strands of Yarn C and hook, ch 18. Cut yarn and tie ends.

Attach strap onto hat front, 1 1/2"/4cm directly above visor. Sew on strap so it is slack in the middle, then sew buttons on either end.

This project was knit with

(A) 1 ball of Lion Wool-Ease Chunky, 80% acrylic/20% wool yarn, bulky weight, 5oz/140g = approx 153yd/140m per ball, color #630-133

(B) 1 ball of Lion Brand Fun Fur, 100% polyester yarn, bulky weight, 1¼oz/50g = approx 60yd/54m, color #194

(C) 1 ball of Lion Wool-Ease Chunky, 80% acrylic/20% wool yarn, bulky weight, 5oz/140g = approx 153yd/140m per ball, color #630-130

Striped Baby Toque

The sensible tie on this hat ensures that it is snugly secured on your toddler's head. It features a delightful striped pattern interspersed with a checkerboard stripe.

EXPERIENCE LEVEL

■■■ ▢ Intermediate

SIZES

Sized for 12 (18, 24) months. Shown in size 12 months.

FINISHED MEASUREMENTS

Around face: 15 (16, 17)"/38 (41, 43)cm

MATERIALS AND TOOLS

For girls

Yarn A **4** : 197yd/180m of Medium weight yarn, acrylic/wool, in deep purple

Yarn B **4** : 197yd/180m of Medium weight yarn, acrylic/wool, in light pink

For boys

Yarn A **4** : 197yd/180m of Medium weight yarn, acrylic/wool, in dark gray

Yarn B **4** : 197yd/180m of Medium weight yarn, acrylic/wool, in light gray

Size 8 (5mm) straight knitting needles OR SIZE TO OBTAIN GAUGE

Two ⅝"/13mm buttons

Yarn needle

GAUGE

In St st, 19 sts and 24 rows to 4"/10cm

In Garter st, 17 sts and 36 rows to 4"/10cm

Measurements

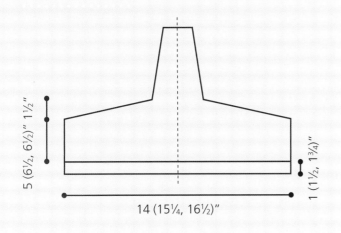

5 (6½, 6½)" 1½"

14 (15¼, 16½)"

1 (1½, 1¾)"

Baby Toque Pattern 1

row 3 2 1

sts 3 2 1

Baby Toque Pattern 2

row 3 2 1

sts 3 2 1

Color and stitch key:

Yarn A ▨ : K on RS and P on WS

Yarn B ■ : K on RS and P on WS

Instructions

COWL

With Yarn A, cast on 66 (72, 78) sts.

Work in Garter st (knit every row) for 6 (8, 10) rows.

STRIPES

*With Yarn A, work in St st for 2 rows.

Join Yarn B. Work in St st for 2 rows.

Rep from * 3 (4, 4) times in all.

BEG BABY TOQUE PATTERN 1

Pat consists of 3 sts and 3 rows.

Work in Baby Toque Pattern 1 on 3 sts, rep pat 22 (24, 26) times on each row.

Cont as established for 3 rows.

*With Yarn B, work in St st for 2 rows.

Join Yarn A. Work in St st for 2 rows.

Rep from * 3 times in all.

BEG BABY TOQUE PATTERN 2

Work as for Baby Toque Pattern 2, reversing yarn colors.

With Yarn A, work in St st for 2 more rows.

*With Yarn B, bind off 5 (5, 6) sts at beg of next 2 rows; work in St st to end.

With Yarn A, bind off 5 (6, 6) sts at beg of next 2 rows; work in St st to end.

Rep from * once more—26 (28, 30) sts.

With Yarn B, work in St st for 2 more rows.

Work in Pat 1 for 3 rows.

*With Yarn B, work in St st for 2 rows.

Join Yarn A. Work in St st for 2 rows.

Rep from * once more.

With Yarn B, bind off 1 st at beg of next 2 rows; work in St st to end.

With Yarn A, work in St st for 2 more rows.

*With Yarn B, work in St st for 2 rows.

Join Yarn A. Work in St st for 2 rows.

Rep from * 2 (3, 3) times in all.

With Yarn B, bind off 1 st at beg of next 2 rows; work in St st to end.

Cont to work in St st for 10 (12, 14) more rows.

Bind off 1 st at beg of next 2 rows; work in St st to end.

Join Yarn A, work in St st for 4 more rows.

Bind off all sts.

FINISHING

Sew back seam.

COLLAR

With Yarn A, cast on 8 sts, with RS facing, insert needle into bottom left corner, pick up and k54 (56, 58) sts evenly spaced (insert needle into each 3rd row st) across bottom.

Work in Garter st for 3 rows.

BUTTONHOLE ROWS

Row 1: K3, bind off 1 st, k to end.

Row 2: K to last 3 sts, cast on 1 st, k3.

Work in Garter st for 5 (7, 9) more rows.

Work buttonhole rows.

Work in Garter st for 3 more rows.

Bind off all sts.

Sew on buttons.

This project was knit with

For girls
(A) 1 ball of Lion Wool-Ease Chunky, 80% acrylic/20% wool yarn, bulky weight, 5oz/140g = approx 153yd/140m per ball, color #630-139

(B) 1 balls of Lion Wool-Ease Chunky, 80% acrylic/20% wool yarn, bulky weight, 5oz/140g = approx 153yd/140m per ball, color #630-104

For boys
(A) 1 ball of Lion Wool-Ease Chunky, 80% acrylic/20% wool yarn, bulky weight, 5oz/140g = approx 153yd/140m per ball, color #630-152

(B) 1 balls of Lion Wool-Ease Chunky, 80% acrylic/20% wool yarn, bulky weight, 5oz/140g = approx 153yd/140m per ball, color #630-151

Miss Muffet's Mittens

These tiny, thumbless mittens will keep fingers warm during baby's first winter. They are excellently matched with Bunny Ear Booties on page 94.

EXPERIENCE LEVEL

■ ■ ■ ☐ Intermediate

SIZES

Sized for newborn–6 months.

FINISHED MEASUREMENTS

Length on arm: above the wrist

MATERIALS AND TOOLS

For girls

Yarn A **4 MEDIUM**: 171yd/156m of Medium weight yarn, cotton, in white

Yarn B **6 SUPER BULKY**: 105yd/96m of Bulky weight yarn, acrylic/nylon, in pink, green and white

For boys

Yarn A **4 MEDIUM**: 171yd/156m of Medium weight yarn, cotton, in white

Yarn B **6 SUPER BULKY**: 105yd/96m of Bulky weight yarn, acrylic/nylon, in blue and white

Size 6 (4mm) straight knitting needles OR SIZE TO OBTAIN GAUGE

Size 6 (4mm) circular knitting needle OR SIZE TO OBTAIN GAUGE

Size F/5 (4mm) crochet hook

Two ⅝"/13mm buttons

Yarn needle

GAUGE

In Garter st, 18 sts and 34 rows to 4"/10cm

Instructions

TOP

(Make 2)

With Yarn A and straight needles, cast on 15 sts.

Rows 1-2: Work in Garter st (knit every row) for 2 rows.

Note: When changing colors, twist yarns tog on WS to prevent holes.

Divide 1 ball of Yarn A into 2. Use one for each edge.

Row 3: With Yarn A, k2, inc 1; with Yarn B, k to last 3 sts; with Yarn A, inc 1, k2—17 sts.

Row 4: With Yarn A, k4; with Yarn B, k to last 4 sts; with Yarn A, k4.

Rows 5-6: Rep rows 3 and 4 once more.

Rows 7–14: Work as for row 4.

Row 15: With Yarn A, k2, k2tog, k1; with Yarn B, k to last 5 sts; with Yarn A, k1, skp, k2—15 sts.

Row 16: With Yarn A, k4; with Yarn B, k to last 4 sts; with Yarn A, k4.

Rep rows 15 and 16 three times in all—11 sts. Cut Yarn B.

With Yarn A only, cont to work in Garter st for 5 more rows, dec 1 st at each side of next and every following 2nd row two times in all—7 sts.

Bind off all sts.

BOTTOM

(Make 2)

With Yarn A and straight needles, cast on 15 sts.

Work in Garter st (knit every row) for 2 rows.

Cont to work in Garter st for 4 more rows, inc 1 st at each side of next and every following 2nd row two times in all—19 sts.

Work in Garter st for 8 more rows.

Cont to work in Garter st for 11 more rows, dec 1 st at each side of next and every following 2nd row 6 times in all—7 sts.

Bind off all sts.

FINISHING

Sew top and bottom parts of mittens tog, leaving cast on edges open.

CUFF

Right mitten

With Yarn A and circular needle, cast on 9 sts, with RS and bottom part of mitten facing, cuff opening away from you, insert needle into first cast on st from your right, pick up and k20 sts evenly spaced around cuff opening—29 sts.

Rows 1-2: Work in Garter st for 2 rows.

Buttonhole rows

Row 3: K to last 3 sts, bind off 1, k1.

Row 4: K2, cast on 1, k to end.

Rows 5-6: Cont to work in Garter st for 2 more rows.

Bind off all sts.

Left mitten

With Yarn A and circular needle, with RS and top part of mitten facing, cuff opening away from you, insert needle into first cast on st from your right, pick up and k20 sts evenly spaced around cuff opening, cast on 9 sts—29 sts.

Rows 1-2: Work in Garter st for 2 rows.

Buttonhole rows

Row 3: K2, bind off 1, k to end.

Row 4: K all to last 2 sts, cast on 1, k2.

Rows 5-6: Cont to work in Garter st for 2 more rows.

Bind off all sts.

Sew on buttons.

RIBBON

With Yarn B and hook, ch 120 sts. Cut yarn and tie ends.

Sew to mittens.

This project was knit with

For girls

(A) 1 ball of Bernat Cottontots, 100% cotton, medium weight yarn, 3½oz/100g = approx 171yd/156m per ball, color #90005

(B) 1 ball of Bernat Baby Bubbles, 53.5% acrylic/46.5% nylon yarn, bulky weight, 2⅖oz/70g = approx 105yd/96m, color #75712

For boys

(A) 1 ball of Bernat Cottontots, 100% cotton yarn, medium weight, 3½oz/100g = approx 171yd/156m per ball, color #90005

(B) 1 ball of Bernat Baby Bubbles, 53.5% acrylic/46.5% nylon yarn, bulky weight, 2⅖oz/70g = approx 105yd/96m, color #75728

Booties Made for Walking

With soft sturdy suede soles, these booties are perfect first-walking shoes. Supple enough to be comfortable and form fitting, they have a sturdy bottom that gives a little traction.

EXPERIENCE LEVEL

■■■□ Intermediate

SIZES

Sized for 12–18 (24) months. Shown in size 24 months.

FINISHED MEASUREMENTS

Length on leg: above ankle

MATERIALS AND TOOLS

Yarn A (6 SUPER BULKY): 153yd/140m of Bulky weight yarn, acrylic/wool, in green

Yarn B (6 SUPER BULKY): 153yd/140m of Bulky weight yarn, acrylic/wool, in amber

Yarn C (6 SUPER BULKY): 60yd/54m of Bulky weight yarn, polyester, in brown

Size 8 (5mm) straight knitting needles OR SIZE TO OBTAIN GAUGE

Size 6 (4mm) 1 set (5) dpn OR SIZE TO OBTAIN GAUGE

Size F/5 (4mm) crochet hook

Tracing paper, pencil, and permanent marker

Scissors

Amber leather square, 8" x 8"/20cm x 20cm

Leather hole punch, 1/8"/3mm hole

Yarn needle

GAUGE

In St st, 18 sts and 28 rows to 4"/10cm

Instructions

CUFF

With Yarn A and straight needles, cast on 24 sts.

*Row 1: K3, p2, work in k2, p2 rib across to last 3 sts, k3.

Row 2: P3, k2, work in p2, k2 rib across to last 3sts, p3.

Rep from * for pat 4 times in all.

LEG

Divide sts evenly between 4 needles—6 sts on each needle.

The space between Needles 1 and 4 is the center of the sock.

Join Yarn B, and work around in St st (k all sts) for 2 rnds.

With Yarn A, work in St st for 1 rnd. Cut Yarn A.

With Yarn B, work in St st for 2 rnds. End at Needle 3.

K1 from Needle 4 onto Needle 3.

UPPER

Using spare needle, k all sts from Needle 4, and 5 sts from Needle 1—10 sts.

Place rem sts from Needle 1 onto Needle 2. Leave sts on Needles 2 and 3 unworked—14 sts in total.

Cut Yarn B.

Join 2 strands of Yarn C, and work back and forth in St st (p1 row, k1 row) for 15 (19) rows. End with WS row.

BASE

Join Yarn A and using spare needle, pick up and k14 (18) sts evenly spaced along right edge of upper. Using same needle, k first 5 sts from working needle. Using other spare needle, k rem 5 sts from working needle, then pick up and k14 (18) sts evenly spaced along left edge of upper.

There are now 52 (60) sts in total: 19 (23) sts each on Needles 1 and 4, and 7 sts on Needles 2 and 3.

Divide sts evenly between 4 needles—13 (15) sts on each needle.

Work-in-the-rnd and k all sts for 6 (8) rnds. Bind off all sts.

FINISHING

Sole

With pencil, copy the appropriate sole template (see page 127) onto tracing paper. Mark ⅛"/3mm holes all around template edge, ¼"/6mm from edge and ¼"/6mm apart from each other. When spacing holes, measure space between each hole from middle of holes. Cut out, transfer to leather square, trace around template with permanent marker, and cut out leather sole. Punch holes as marked.

Position sole on bottom of slipper. Orient leather with smooth side upwards, so that child doesn't slip while walking. Secure sole in place with loose stitches in several places.

Thread needle with Yarn B and sew sole to the slipper with overlap stitches through sole holes and slipper.

Cords and crocheted edging

With Yarn B and hook, ch 40 for first cord.

With RS facing and toe to the left, insert hook in closest corner st of cuff opening. Sl st, sc 1 into each st around cuff opening.

Ch 40 for the 2nd cord.

Cut yarn and tie ends.

Knot ends of each cord.

This project was knit with

(A) 1 ball of Lion Wool-Ease Chunky, 80% acrylic/20% wool yarn, bulky weight, 5oz/140g = approx 153yd/140m per ball, color #630-130

(B) 1 ball of Lion Wool-Ease Chunky, 80% acrylic/20% wool yarn, bulky weight, 5oz/140g = approx 153yd/140m per ball, color #630-186

(C) 1 ball of Lion Brand Fun Fur, 100% polyester yarn, bulky weight, 1¼oz/50g = approx 60yd/54m per ball, color #134

Bunny Ear Booties

These adorable booties will keep baby's feet warm and cozy. They are perfectly matched with Miss Muffet's Mittens on page 86.

EXPERIENCE LEVEL

■■■□ Intermediate

SIZES

Sized for newborn (3, 6 months).

FINISHED MEASUREMENTS

Length on leg: above ankle

MATERIALS AND TOOLS

For girls

Yarn A **MEDIUM 4**: 171yd/156m of Medium weight yarn, cotton, in white

Yarn B **SUPER BULKY 6**: 105yd/96m of Bulky weight yarn, acrylic/nylon, in pink, green and white

For boys

Yarn A **MEDIUM 4**: 171yd/156m of Medium weight yarn, cotton, in white

Yarn B **SUPER BULKY 6**: 105yd/96m of Bulky weight yarn, acrylic/nylon, in blue and white

Size 3 (3mm) straight knitting needles OR SIZE TO OBTAIN GAUGE

Size E/4 (3.5mm) crochet hook

Two Stitch holders

Two ⅝"/13mm buttons

Yarn needle

GAUGE

In Garter st, 20 sts and 36 rows to 4"/10cm

Instructions

SOLE

With Yarn A, cast on 31 (37, 43) sts.

Work in Garter st for 2 rows.

Mark middle st.

For making sole roundish:

Cont to work in Garter st for 7 more rows, inc 1 st at each edge and 1 st at each side from middle st, next and every following 2nd row 4 times in all—47 (53, 59) sts.

Cont to work in Garter st for 7 (9, 11) more rows.

INSTEP

Place first 20 (22, 24) sts onto right needle. With Yarn B, work 7 (9, 11) middle sts as follows:

*K6 (8, 10), k2tog; turn. Rep from * 12 (14, 16) times in all—35 (39, 43) sts.

With Yarn A, cont to work in Garter st on all 35 (39, 43) sts, for 2 rows.

LEG OPENING AND EARS

Place first 10 (12, 13) sts onto holder, bind off next 5 sts for opening, place middle 7 (7, 9) sts onto holder, bind off next 5 sts for opening, place last 10 (12, 13) onto holder.

Work middle 7 (7, 9) sts as follows:

With Yarn B, work in Garter st for 2 rows.

Next Row: K3 (3, 4) for ear, bind off 1, k2 (2, 3) for ear

Work in Garter st for 11 (11, 13) more rows, for each ear separately.

Bind off all sts.

CUFF

Right bootie

RS: Place last 10 (12, 13) sts from holder back onto needle; with Yarn A, work in Garter st for 8 (8, 10) rows.

Bind off all sts.

WS: Place first 10 (12, 13) sts from holder back onto needle; with Yarn A, work in Garter st for 1 (1, 3) rows.

STRAP

Next row (RS): K to end, cast on 11 (13, 15) sts.

Work in Garter st for 2 rows.

Buttonhole rows

Row 1: K to last 3 sts, bind off 1, k1.

Row 2: K2, cast on 1, k to end.

Cont to work in Garter st for 2 more rows.

Bind off all sts.

Left bootie

WS: Place first 10 (12, 13) sts from holder back onto needle; with Yarn A, work in Garter st for 7 (7, 9) rows.

Bind off all sts.

WS: Place last 10 (12, 13) sts from holder back onto needle; with Yarn A, work in Garter st for 2 rows.

STRAP

Work same as for right bootie.

FINISHING

Sew back and sole in one continuous seam.

Sew on buttons.

CROCHETED EDGING

With RS facing and Yarn A, insert hook into back seam of cuff edge, ch 1, then sc 1 evenly across cuff opening, sc 3 into corner, cont down to ears, then across both ears to strap, along strap bottom, sc 3 into corner, up to next corner, sc 3 into corner, along strap top and cuff opening.

Join with sl st and fasten off.

This project was knit with

For girls
(A) 1 ball of Bernat Cottontots, 100% cotton yarn, medium weight, 3½oz/100g = approx 171yd/156m per ball, color #90005

(B) 1 ball of Bernat Baby Bubbles, 53.5% acrylic/46.5% nylon yarn, bulky weight, 2⅖oz/70g = approx 105yd/96m, color #75712

For boys
A) 1 ball of Bernat Cottontots, 100% cotton yarn, medium weight, 3½oz/100g = approx 171yd/156m per ball, color #90005

(B) 1 ball of Bernat Baby Bubbles, 53.5% acrylic/46.5% nylon yarn, bulky weight, 2⅖oz/70g = approx 105yd/96m, color #75128

Super Striped Socks

With funky bright stripes and perfectly round pompons, feet will be dancing when they don this design. Note that each sock uses different color yarns for the cuffs, heels, toes, and pompons.

EXPERIENCE LEVEL

■■■□ Intermediate

SIZES

Sized for 3 (6–12, 18–24) months. Shown in size 6–12 months.

FINISHED MEASUREMENTS

Length on leg: mid-calf

MATERIALS AND TOOLS

Yarn MC **3 LIGHT**: 147yd/135m of Light weight yarn, acrylic, in pink, yellow, green, white and blue

Yarn A **4 MEDIUM**: 207yd/188m of Medium weight yarn, cotton/acrylic, in light green

Yarn B **4 MEDIUM**: 207yd/188m of Medium weight yarn, cotton/acrylic, in yellow

Yarn C **4 MEDIUM**: 207yd/188m of Medium weight yarn, cotton/acrylic, in burnt orange

Size 4 (3.5mm) 1 set (5) dpn OR SIZE TO OBTAIN GAUGE

Size E/4 (3.5mm) crochet hook

Tracing paper, pencil, and permanent marker

Scissors

Large piece of cardboard

Yarn needle

GAUGE

With Yarn MC, in St st, 23 sts and 32 rows to 4"/10cm

Instructions

CUFF

With Yarn A (B), cast on 24 (28,32) sts.

Divide sts evenly between 4 needles—6 (7, 8) sts on each needle.

Join, taking care not to twist sts on needles.

The space between Needles 1 and 4 is the center of the sock.

Work around in k1, p1 rib for 15 (15, 19) rnds.

Cut Yarn A (B).

LEG

Join MC Yarn, and work around in St st (k all sts) for 15 (25, 27) rnds.

End at Needle 3.

Don't cut yarn (you'll be using it again to work the gusset).

HEEL FLAP

Join Yarn B (C) and using spare needle, sl 1, k across sts from Needle 4, then Needle 1—11 (13, 15) sts; leave sts on Needles 2 and 3 unworked.

Work back and forth in St st (k1 row, p1 row) for 7 (9, 11) more rows.

End with WS row.

HEEL

Work short rows as follows:

Sl 1, k7 (8, 10), skp, turn;

*Sl 1, p4 (4, 6), p2tog, turn;

sl 1, k4 (4, 6), skp, turn.

Rep from * until all sts have been worked—6 (6, 8) sts.

Cut Yarn B (C).

Next row (RS) With MC Yarn, k3 (3, 4) sts onto Needle 4, then k3 (3, 4) sts onto Needle 1.

GUSSET

Using Needle 1, insert needle into first k st from edge, and pick up and k6 (8, 8) sts evenly spaced along edge of heel.

Note: When forming gusset, avoid holes between corner of heel flap and leg in the following manner: For the last stitch that you pick up, insert needle into 2nd row stitch under first stitch on Needle 2. For the first st that you pick up, insert needle into 2nd row stitch under the first sts on Needle 4.

Cont to work in-the-rnd and k sts on Needles 2 and 3.

Using spare needle, pick up and k6 (8, 10) sts evenly spaced along edge of heel, then k3 (3, 4) sts from Needle 4—9 (11, 12) sts on Needles 1 and 4.

INSTEP

*Rnd 1: K all sts.

Rnd 2: Needle 1: K to last 3 sts, skp, k1; Needles 2 and 3: K all sts; Needle 4: K1, k2tog, k to end.

Rep from * until there are 6 (7, 8) sts on Needles 1 and 4—24 (28, 32) sts in total.

FOOT

Work around in k for 12 (20, 26) rnds.

Cut MC Yarn.

TOE

Join Yarn C (A).

*Rnd 1: K all sts.

Rnd 2 (dec rnd): Needles 1 and 3: K to last 3 sts, skp, k1; Needles 2 and 4: K1, k2tog, k to end.

Rep from * until 4 (5, 5) sts rem on each needle.

Now rep rnd 2 every rnd until 2 sts rem on each needle.

Cut yarn, leaving a 10"/25cm tail.

Thread the needle with the tail and *insert through all sts, from first to last.

Draw yarn back through all sts and tighten. Rep from * twice.

Cut yarn and tie ends.

POMPONS

(Make 2)

Make 1 using Yarn B and 1 using Yarn C (see Pompon Template 2, page 127).

RIBBON

Insert hook into tie at middle of pompon, and with 2 strands of Yarn B (C) ch 10. Cut yarn and tie ends.

Thread the tails from the ribbon onto the needle and sew the pompon at back middle onto the WS of sock, under the cuff.

This project was knit with

(MC) 1 ball of Moda Dea Sassy Stripes, 100% acrylic yarn, light weight, 1¾oz/50g = approx 147yd/135m, color #6983

(A) 1 ball of Lion Cotton Ease, 100% cotton yarn, medium weight, 3½oz/100g = approx 171yd/156m color #830-194

(B) 1 ball of Lion Cotton Ease, 100% cotton yarn, medium weight, 3½oz/100g = approx 171yd/156m color #830-186

(C) 1 ball of Lion Cotton Ease, 100% cotton yarn, medium weight, 3½oz/100g = approx 171yd/156m color #830-134

Fluffy Horned Hat

With its fabulous fluffy horns, this design is perfect for keeping hat on the heads of kids who generally like taking hats off!

EXPERIENCE LEVEL

▰▰▱▱▱ Intermediate

SIZES

Sized for newborn–3 months (6, 12 months). Shown in size Newborn–3 months.

FINISHED MEASUREMENTS

Head circumference 14 (16, 18)"/35.5 (40.5, 45.5)cm

MATERIALS AND TOOLS

For girls

Yarn A  : 171yd/156m of Medium weight yarn, cotton, in white

Yarn B **6** SUPER BULKY : 105yd/96m of Bulky weight yarn, acrylic/nylon, in pink, green and white

For boys

Yarn A **4** MEDIUM : 171yd/156m of Medium weight yarn, cotton, in white

Yarn B **6** SUPER BULKY : 105yd/96m of Bulky weight yarn, acrylic/nylon, in blue and white

Size 6 (4mm) straight knitting needles OR SIZE TO OBTAIN GAUGE
Size 8 (5mm) circular knitting needle OR SIZE TO OBTAIN GAUGE

Stitch holder

Yarn needle

GAUGE

In St st, 18 sts and 27 rows to 4"/10cm

Instructions

BACK

With Yarn A, cast on 34 (39, 44) sts.

Work in k2, p2 rib for 16 (22, 28) rows.

*Work in St st for 4 rows.

Join Yarn B. Work in St st for 2 rows.

Rep from * 3 times in all.

Work in St st for 8 (10, 12) more rows.

Next Row: K10 for right horn, bind off 14 (19, 24) center sts, k10 for left horn.

Work each horn separately.

Leave rem sts for right horn on a holder.

LEFT HORN

Cont to work in St st for 35 more rows, beg with WS row; at the same time, dec 1 st at each side every 12th row twice—6 sts.

Bind off all sts.

RIGHT HORN

Work same as for left horn.

FRONT

Work to correspond to back, reversing horns.

Use Yarn B for horns.

FINISHING

Sew hat side seams and horns seams. Sew hat top seam (between horns).

This project was knit with

For girls
(A) 1 ball of Bernat Cottontots, 100% cotton yarn, medium weight, 3½oz/100g = approx 171yd/156m per ball, color #90005

(B) 1 ball of Bernat Baby Bubbles, 53.5% acrylic/46.5% nylon yarn, bulky weight, 2⅖oz/70g = approx 105yd/96m, color #75712

For boys
(A) 1 ball of Bernat Cottontots, 100% cotton yarn, medium weight, 3½oz/100g = approx 171yd/156m per ball, color #90005

(B) 1 ball of Bernat Baby Bubbles, 53.5% acrylic/46.5% nylon yarn, bulky weight, 2⅖oz/70g = approx 105yd/96m, color #75128

Huggable Snuggable Bunny

This floppy bunny loves to be hugged and snuggled. Soft and soothing to the touch, it's a lovely knitted companion in any baby's bed.

EXPERIENCE LEVEL

■■■ □ Intermediate

FINISHED MEASUREMENTS

Approx 17"/43cm tall

MATERIALS AND TOOLS

Yarn A **MEDIUM 4**: 103yd/94m of Medium weight yarn, organic cotton, in dusty light beige

Yarn B **MEDIUM 4**: 103yd/94m of Medium weight yarn, organic cotton, in natural white

Yarn C **MEDIUM 4**: 103yd/94m of Medium weight yarn, organic cotton, in dark brown

Size 8 (5mm) straight knitting needles OR SIZE TO OBTAIN GAUGE

Two ⅜"/10mm buttons

1 pound polyester fiberfill stuffing

Yarn needle

GAUGE

In St st, 15 sts and 23 rows to 4"/10cm

Instructions

BODY

(Beg at base)

With Yarn A, cast on 16 sts loosely.

Row 1 and all WS rows: P all sts.

Row 2: Inc K wise into every st—32 sts.

Rows 3-5: Beg with a WS row, work in St st for 3 rows.

Row 6: Inc K wise into every st—64 sts.

CHEST PANEL

Note: When changing colors, twist yarns tog on WS to prevent holes.

Divide 1 ball of Yarn A in half. Use one half for each edge.

Row 8: With Yarn A, k22, join Yarn B, and k20, join Yarn A and k22.

Row 9: With Yarn A, p22, with Yarn B, p20, with Yarn A, p22.

Rows 10-25: Rep rows 8 and 9, 8 times more.

BACK SHAPING

Row 26: With Yarn A, k2, k2tog, k19, with Yarn B k18, with Yarn A k to last 4 sts, SKP, k2.

Row 27: With Yarn A, p22, with Yarn B, p18, with Yarn A, p22.

Rows 28-29: Work in St st for 2 rows.

Row 30: With Yarn A, k2, k2tog, k19, with Yarn B k16, with Yarn A k to last 4 sts, SKP, k2.

Row 31: With Yarn A, p22, with Yarn B, p16, with Yarn A, p22.

Rows 32-33: Work in St st for 2 rows.

Row 34: With Yarn A, k2, k2tog, k19, with Yarn B k14, with Yarn A k to last 4 sts, SKP, k2.

Row 35: With Yarn A, p22, with Yarn B, p14, with Yarn A, p22.

Rows 36-37: Work in St st for 2 rows.

Row 38: With Yarn A, k2, k2tog, k19, with Yarn B k12, with Yarn A k to last 4 sts, SKP, k2.

Row 39: With Yarn A, p22, with Yarn B, p12, with Yarn A, p22.

Rows 40-41: Work in St st for 2 rows.

Row 42: With Yarn A, k2, k2tog, k19, with Yarn B k10, with Yarn A k to last 4 sts, SKP, k2.

Row 43: With Yarn A, p22, with Yarn B, p10, with Yarn A, p22.

Rows 44-45: Work in St st for 2 rows.

Row 46: With Yarn A, k2, k2tog, k19, with Yarn B k8, with Yarn A k to last 4 sts, SKP, k2.

Row 47: With Yarn A, p22, with Yarn B, p8, with Yarn A, p22.

Rows 48-49: Work in St st for 2 rows.

Cut Yarn B.

Work in St st for 4 more rows, dec 1 st at each side of next and every following row twice—48 sts.

Next row: (K2tog) to end.

Bind off all sts.

Sew center back seam. Run thread through cast on sts, draw up tightly, and fasten off. Fill firmly, leaving neck edge open.

HEAD

(Beg at neck edge)

With Yarn A, cast on 24 sts.

Rows 1-3: Beg with a WS row, work in St st for 3 rows.

Row 4: K4, inc K wise into next 16 sts, k4—40 sts.

Rows 5-25: Work in St st for 21 rows.

Row 26: K4, *k2 tog, rep from * 16 times, k4—24 sts.

Row 27: P to end.

Row 28: (K2tog) to end—12 sts.

Cut yarn, leaving a 10"/25cm tail. Thread needle with tail and *insert through all sts, from first to last. Draw yarn back through all sts and tighten.

Sew center back seam. Fill firmly and sew head to body, placing back seam of head to back seam of body.

EARS

(Make 2, beg at lower edge)

Outer ear

With Yarn A, cast on 12 sts.

Beg with a WS row, work in St st for 11 rows.

Work in St st for 24 more rows, dec 1 st at each side of Rows 12, 22, 30, 36—4 sts.

Work in P for 1 row.

Cut Yarn A.

Inner ear

Join Yarn B.

Work in St st for 24 more rows, inc 1 st at each side of Rows 38, 44, 52, 62—12 sts.

Work in St st for 11 rows.

Bind off all sts.

Sew ears side and base edges together. Sew ears on top of head.

LEGS

(Make 2, beg at lower edge)

With Yarn A, cast on 10 sts.

Row 1: P all sts.

Row 2: Inc K wise into every st—20 sts.

Beg with a WS row, work in St st for 19 more rows.

Next Row: (K2tog) to end—10 sts.

Work in P for 1 row.

Next Row: (K2tog) to end—5 sts.

Cut yarn, leaving a 10"/25cm tail. Thread needle with tail and *insert through all sts, from first to last. Draw yarn back through all sts and tighten.

Sew row ends together, leaving a gap near to top edge of back seam. Run thread through cast on sts, draw up tightly and fasten off. Fill firmly, sew gap in seam and sew legs to lower side edges of body with Whip st.

ARMS

(Make 2, beg at lower edge)

With Yarn A, cast on 10 sts.

Row 1: P all sts.

Row 2: Inc K wise into every st—20 sts.

Beg with a WS row, work in St st for 17 more rows.

Cont to work in St st for 10 more rows, dec 1 st at each side of next and every following row 5 times—10 sts.

Next Row: (K2tog) to end—5 sts.

Cut yarn, leaving a 10"/25cm tail. Thread needle with tail and *insert through all sts, from first to last. Draw yarn back through all sts and tighten.

Sew row ends together, leaving a gap near to top edge back seam. Run thread through cast on sts, draw up tightly and fasten off. Fill firmly, sew gap in seam and sew arms to upper side edges of body, about 2 rows below neck seam.

TAIL

With Yarn B, cast on 8 sts.

Row 1: P all sts.

Row 2: Inc K wise into every st—16 sts

Beg with a WS row, work in St st for 9 more rows.

Next Row: (K2tog) to end—8 sts.

Cut yarn, leaving a 10"/25cm tail. Thread the needle with the tail and *insert through all sts, from first to last. Draw yarn back through all sts, then gather round all other edges.

Fill firmly, draw up gathers tightly and fasten off. Sew tail to body back seam, about 2¾"/7cm above body base.

SCARF

With Yarn C, cast on 8 sts.

Work in St st for 70 rows.

Make 5 fringes at each end.

Bind off all sts.

FINISHING

With Yarn C, embroider nose using Satin stitch. Position eyes above nose, and sew on.

This project was knit with

(A) 2 balls of Lion Nature's Choice Organic Cotton, organic cotton yarn, medium weight, 3oz/85g = approx 103yd/94m, color #480-099

(B) 1 ball of Lion Nature's Choice Organic Cotton, organic cotton yarn, medium weight, 3oz/85g = approx 103yd/94m, color #480-098

(C) 1 ball of Lion Nature's Choice Organic Cotton, organic cotton yarn, medium weight, 3oz/85g = approx 103yd/94m, color #480-125

Six-Sided Soft Toy

Each side of this toy is knitted separately, and features different colors and patterns. With a truck, a tree, a house, a boat, a fish, and a pair of children, there's something for everyone!

EXPERIENCE LEVEL

■■■ ☐ Intermediate

FINISHED MEASUREMENTS

Approx 5½" x 5½" x 5½"/14cm x 14cm x 14cm

MATERIALS AND TOOLS

Yarn A **MEDIUM 4**: 178yd/163m of Medium weight yearn, cotton/acrylic, in light yellow

Yarn B **MEDIUM 4**: 178yd/163m of Medium weight yearn, cotton/acrylic, in light green

Yarn C **MEDIUM 4**: 178yd/163m of Medium weight yearn, cotton/acrylic, in light orange

Yarn D **MEDIUM 4**: 178yd/163m of Medium weight yearn, cotton/acrylic, in green

Yarn E **MEDIUM 4**: 178yd/163m of Medium weight yearn, cotton/acrylic, in light blue

Yarn F **MEDIUM 4**: 178yd/163m of Medium weight yearn, cotton/acrylic, in light purple

Size 6 (4mm) straight knitting needles OR SIZE TO OBTAIN GAUGE

Size E/4 (3.5mm) crochet hook

Rem yarns and felt

Yarn needle

½ pound polyester fiberfill stuffing

Small bells, optional

GAUGE

In St st, 20 sts and 28 rows to 4"/10cm

Instructions

SQUARES

(Make 1 of each)

See opposite page, and pages 117 to 119, for patterns.

Truck square (Yarn A)

Tree square (Yarn B)

House square (Yarn C)

Boat square (Yarn D)

Fish square (Yarn E)

Children's square (Yarn F)

Each square consists of 30 sts and 36 rows.

With appropriate yarn for each square, cast on 30 sts.

Work in St st (k1 row, p1 row) until row when pat starts (different row for each pat).

Work in pat the number of rows necessary for different squares.

Cont to work in St st until 36 rows in all are completed. Bind off all sts.

FINISHING

Decorating

To decorate squares using rem yarns from other projects, simply trace pat shape using contrasting color yarn with Running stitch. Attach felt onto some shapes to make girl's dress, boy's shorts, boat's sail, or truck's wheels, using same Running stitch.

To make braids for girl, insert hook through st where you want braid to begin, fold Yarn A (or any other yarn) in half, pull yarn through and with 2 strands, ch 5. Cut yarn and tie ends.

Using contrasting yarn and following diagram, sew squares tog using whip sts to connect square edges, leaving an opening for stuffing. Stuff firmly (you can add small bells if you want), then sew opening closed.

This project was knit with

(A) 1 ball of TLC Cotton Plus, 51% cotton/49% acrylic yarn, medium weight yarn, 3½oz/100g = approx 178yd/163m per ball, color #3222

(B) 1 ball of TLC Cotton Plus, 51% cotton/49% acrylic yarn, medium weight yarn, 3½oz/100g = approx 178yd/163m per ball, color #3643

(C) 1 ball of TLC Cotton Plus, 51% cotton/49% acrylic yarn, medium weight yarn, 3½oz/100g = approx 178yd/163m per ball, color #3252

(D) 1 ball of TLC Cotton Plus, 51% cotton/49% acrylic yarn, medium weight yarn, 3½oz/100g = approx 178yd/163m per ball, color #3645

(E) 1 ball of TLC Cotton Plus, 51% cotton/49% acrylic yarn, medium weight yarn, 3½oz/100g = approx 178yd/163m per ball, color #3811

(F) 1 ball of TLC Cotton Plus, 51% cotton/49% acrylic yarn, medium weight yarn, 3½oz/100g = approx 178yd/163m per ball, color #3590

Children's Square Pattern

row

36

30

20

10

1

sts 30   20   10   1

Color and stitch key:

■ : K on RS rows and P on WS rows

■ : P on RS rows and K on WS rows

Cube Placement Diagram

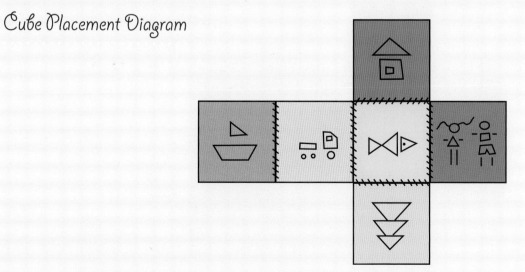

Vintage Blanket

The comforting blanket consists of 45 separate squares that are sewn together. The squares are made in five different colors and use five different patterns. Making it is a labor of love that is sure to be rewarded with years of snuggling.

EXPERIENCE LEVEL

Easy

FINISHED MEASUREMENTS

Approx 30" x 54"/75cm x 135cm

MATERIALS AND TOOLS

Yarn A **MEDIUM 4**: 356yd/326m of Medium weight yarn, cotton/acrylic, in light yellow

Yarn B **MEDIUM 4**: 356yd/326m of Medium weight yarn, cotton/acrylic, in light green

Yarn C **MEDIUM 4**: 356yd/326m of Medium weight yarn, cotton/acrylic, in light orange

Yarn D **MEDIUM 4**: 356yd/326m of Medium weight yarn, cotton/acrylic, in light blue

Yarn E **MEDIUM 4**: 356yd/326m of Medium weight yarn, cotton/acrylic, in red, orange, blue, green and white

Size 8 (5mm) straight knitting needles OR SIZE TO OBTAIN GAUGE

Size E/4 (3.5mm) crochet hook

Yarn needle

GAUGE

In St st, 19 sts and 25 rows to 4"/10cm

Instructions

Make a total of 45 of the following:

Make 45 squares, in the following patterns and colors:

Track squares—2 (Yarn A), 2 (Yarn B), 2 (Yarn C), 2 (Yarn D);

House squares—2 (Yarn A), 2 (Yarn B), 2 (Yarn C), 2 (Yarn D);

Tree squares—2 (Yarn A), 2 (Yarn B), 2 (Yarn C), 2 (Yarn D);

Boat squares—2 (Yarn A), 2 (Yarn B), 2 (Yarn C), 2 (Yarn D);

Fish squares—1 (Yarn A), 1 (Yarn B), 1 (Yarn C), 1 (Yarn D).

SQUARES

Each square consists of 30 sts and 36 rows.

Basic square

With Yarn E, cast on 30 sts.

Work in St st (k1 row, p1 row) for 36 rows. Bind off all sts.

For all other squares, work as for Basic square until pat starts. Work the number of pat rows necessary for different squares. Cont to work as for Basic square.

FINISHING

Follow placement diagram and using Yarn A, sew squares tog in rows, then connect the rows, using whip sts to connect square edges. Using Yarn C and needle, make crosses on each four square junction.

CROCHETED EDGING

With RS facing and Yarn A, insert hook into blanket corner, ch 3, sk, sl st under edge st, *ch 2, sk, sl st under edge st. Rep from * around border. Join and fasten off.

This project was knit with

(A) 2 balls of TLC Cotton Plus, 51% cotton/49% acrylic yarn, medium weight yarn, 3½oz/100g = approx 178yd/163m per ball, color #3222

(B) 2 balls of TLC Cotton Plus, 51% cotton/49% acrylic yarn, medium weight yarn, 3½oz/100g = approx 178yd/163m per ball, color #3643

(C) 2 balls of TLC Cotton Plus, 51% cotton/49% acrylic yarn, medium weight yarn, 3½oz/100g = approx 178yd/163m per ball, color #3252

(D) 2 balls of TLC Cotton Plus, 51% cotton/49% acrylic yarn, medium weight yarn, 3½oz/100g = approx 178yd/163m per ball, color #3645

(E) 2 balls of TLC Cotton Plus, 51% cotton/49% acrylic yarn, medium weight yarn, 3½oz/100g = approx 178yd/163m per ball, color #3615

Truck Square Pattern

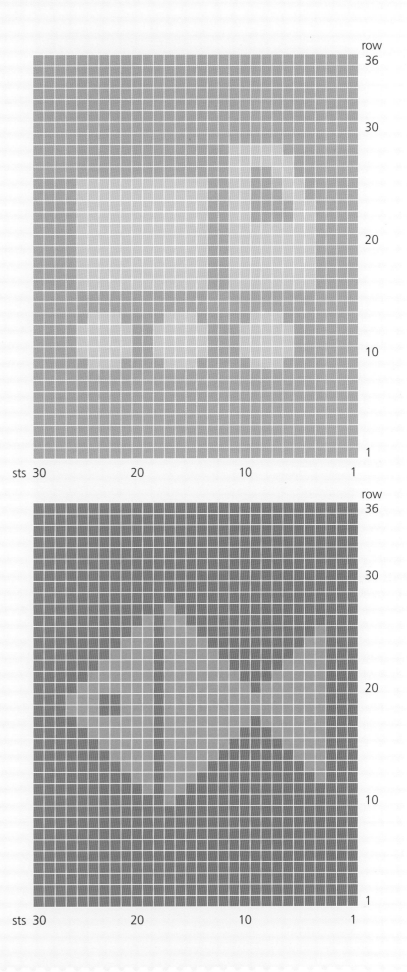

Color and stitch key:

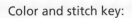 : K on RS rows and P on WS rows

: P on RS rows and K on WS rows

row 36

30

20

10

1

sts 30   20   10   1

Fish Square Pattern

Color and stitch key:

: K on RS rows and P on WS rows

: P on RS rows and K on WS rows

row 36

30

20

10

1

sts 30   20   10   1

House Square Pattern

Color and stitch key:

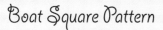 : K on RS rows and P on WS rows

: P on RS rows and K on WS rows

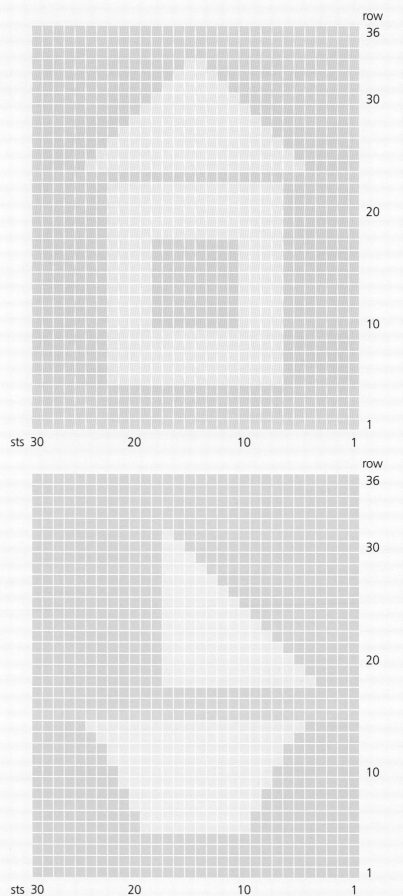

Tree Square Pattern

Color and stitch key:

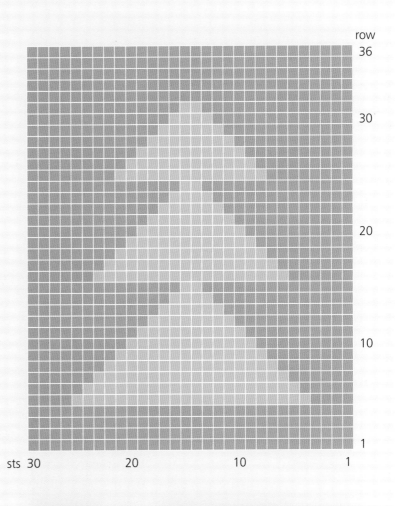

■ : K on RS rows and P on WS rows

■ : P on RS rows and K on WS rows

Blanket Placement Diagram

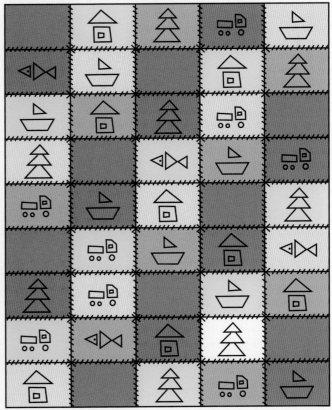

Sleeping Bag with Hood

This button-up blanket is perfect for wrapping a newborn baby. The closed bottom keeps the heat in, while the open top gives baby plenty of peeking space.

EXPERIENCE LEVEL

▬▬▬▭ Intermediate

SIZES

Sized for newborn–6 months.

FINISHED MEASUREMENTS

Chest at underarm 26"/66cm

Length 20"/51cm

Sleeve width at upper arm 11½"/29cm

MATERIALS AND TOOLS

Yarn A (SUPER BULKY 6): 324yd/294m of Bulky weight yarn, polyester, in white

Size 10 1/2 (6.5mm) straight knitting needles OR SIZE TO OBTAIN GAUGE

Stitch holder

Size J/10 (6mm) crochet hook

Seven 3/4"/20mm buttons

Yarn needle

GAUGE

In St st, 10 sts and 16 rows to 4"/10cm

Measurements

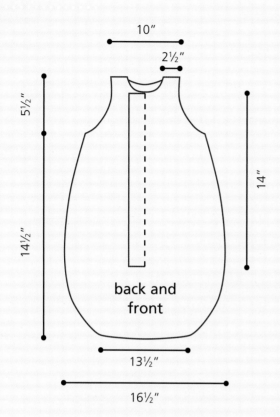

10"

2½"

5½"

14"

14½"

back and front

13½"

16½"

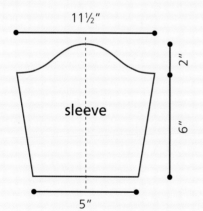

11½"

2"

sleeve

6"

5"

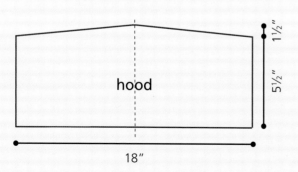

1½"

hood

5½"

18"

Instructions

BACK

Cast on 36 sts.

Work in Garter st for 2 rows.

Cont to work in Garter st for 6 more rows, inc 1 st, at each side every 2nd row 3 times—42 sts.

*Work in St st for 5 rows.

Work in knit for 1 row. End with WS row.

Rep from * twice.

*Work in St st for 7 rows, dec 1 st, at each side of first row.

Work in knit for 1 row. End with WS row.

Rep from * 6 times, total—30 sts.

Work in Garter st for 2 rows.

ARMHOLE SHAPING

Bind off 2 sts at beg of next 2 rows; work in Garter st to end.

Bind off 1 st at beg of next 4 rows; work in Garter st to end—22 sts.

Cont to work in Garter st for 12 more rows.

BACK NECK SHAPING

Row 1: K6, bind off center 10 sts for neck, k to end.

Work separately.

Rows 2-3: Work in Garter st for 2 rows for each shoulder.

Bind off all sts.

FRONT

With WS of back facing and bottom away, pick up and k36 sts along bottom, inserting needle into each cast on st.

Work in Garter st for 2 rows.

Cont to work in Garter st for 6 more rows, inc 1 st at each side every 2nd row 3 times—42 sts.

Work in St st for 5 rows.

(WS): Work in knit for 1 row.

LEFT FRONT

Work on first 26 sts as follows, placing rem 16 sts onto holder.

Row 1: K to end.

Row 2: K5 for border, p to end.

Rows 3-4: Rep rows 1 and 2 once.

Rows 5-6: Rep row 1 twice.

Buttonhole rows

Row 7: K2, k2tog, k to last 3 sts, bind off 1, k1.

Row 8: K2, cast on 1, k2, p to end—25 sts.

Rows 9–12: Rep rows 1 and 2 twice.

Rows 13–14: Rep row 1 twice

Row 15: K2, k2tog, k to end—24 sts.

Row 16: Rep row 2 once.

Buttonhole rows

Row 17: K to last 3 sts, bind off 1, k1.

Row 18: K2, cast on 1, k2, p to end.

Rows 19–20: Rep rows 1 and 2 once.

Rows 21–22: Rep row 1 twice.

Row 23: Rep row 15 once—23 sts.

Row 24: Rep row 2 once.

Rows 25–26: Rep rows 1 and 2 once.

Buttonhole rows

Rows 27–28: Rep rows 7 and 8 once—22 sts.

Rows 29–30: Rep rows 1 and 2 once.

Row 31: Rep row 15 once—21 sts.

Row 32: Rep row 2 once.

Rows 33–36: Rep rows 1 and 2 twice.

Buttonhole rows

Rows 37–38: Rep rows 17 and 18 once.

Row 39: Rep row 15 once—20 sts.

Row 40: Rep row 2 once.

Rows 41–46: Rep rows 1 and 2 three times.

Buttonhole rows

Rows 47–48: Rep rows 17 and 18 once—19 sts.

Work in Garter st for 2 rows.

LEFT ARMHOLE SHAPING

Row 1: Bind off 2, k to end.

Row 2, 4: K to end.

Rows 3, 5: Bind off 1, k to end—16 sts.

Row 6: Work in Garter st for 1 row.

Buttonhole rows

Row 7: K to last 3 sts, bind off 1, k1.

Row 8: K2, cast on 1, k2, k to end.

Work in Garter st for 3 rows.

LEFT NECK SHAPING

Row 1(WS): Bind off 5 sts, work in Garter st to end—11 sts.

Rows 2-4: Work in Garter st for 3 rows.

Row 5: Bind off 2 sts, work in Garter st to end—9 sts.

Row 6: Work in Garter st for 1 row.

Rows 7-8: Rep rows 5 and 6 once—7 sts.

Row 9: Bind off 1 st, work in Garter st to end—6 sts.

Work in Garter st for 1 row.

Bind off rem sts.

RIGHT FRONT

Place last 16 sts from holder back onto needle.

Row 1: Cast on 5 sts for border, k to end—21 sts.

Row 2 (WS): P to last 5 sts, k to end.

Row 3: K to end.

Rows 4-5: Rep rows 2 and 3 once.

Row 6 (WS): K to end.

*Row 7 (RS): K to last 4 sts, skp, k to end—20 sts.

Row 8: P to last 5 sts, k to end for border.

Row 9: K to end.

Rows 10-13: Rep rows 2 and 3 twice.

Row 14 (WS): K to end.

Rows 15-46: Rep from * 4 more times—15 sts.

Row 47: K to end.

Row 48: P to last 5 sts, k to end for border.

Work in Garter st for 2 rows.

RIGHT ARMHOLE SHAPING

Row 1: K to end.

Row 2: Bind off 2, k to end—13 sts.

Rows 3: K to end.

Row 4: Bind off 1, k to end—12 sts.

Rows 5-8: Rep rows 3 and 4 twice—11 sts.

Cont to work in Garter st for 10 more rows.

RIGHT NECK SHAPING

Row 1 (RS): Bind off 2 sts, work in Garter st to end—9 sts.

Row 2: Work in Garter st for 1 row.

Rows 3-4: Rep rows 1 and 2 once—7 sts.

Row 5: Bind off 1 st, work in Garter st to end—6 sts.

Bind off all sts.

SLEEVES

Cast on 18 sts.

Work in Garter st for 6 rows.

*Work in St st for 3 rows, inc 1 st at each side of first row—20 sts.

(WS): Work in knit for 1 row.

Rep from * 5 more times—30 sts.

SLEEVE TOP SHAPING

Bind off 2 sts at beg of next 4 rows; work in Garter st to end—22 sts.

Bind off 1 st at beg of next 2 rows; work in Garter st to end—20 sts.

Bind off all sts.

HOOD

Cast on 56 sts

Work in Garter st for 4 rows.

*Work in St st for 5 rows.

(WS): K for 1 row.

Rep from * 3 times.

Bind off 4 sts at beg of next 6 rows; work in Garter st to end—32 sts.

Bind off all sts.

FINISHING

Sew shoulder seams. Sew sleeve seams. Sew on right front border bottom.

Sew side seams, using hook as follows:

With RS facing, front facing, and bottom at your left, insert hook into lower armhole corner (front and back both), ch 1, sc 1 under edge sts along right seam to bottom corner, sc 2 into corner, cont across bottom, inserting hook into cast on sts, sc 2 into corner, and along left seam up to armhole opening. End with sl st.

Set in sleeves sewing last ¼"/6mm at top of sleeve to bound-off armhole sts.

Sew hood back seam. With WS of hood and bag facing, attach hood to neck opening, sewing it on 7 sts to the left from top left edge all around neck opening to top right edge.

CROCHETED EDGING

With RS and front facing, bottom at your left, insert hook into top left corner, under the hood, ch 5 for button loop, sc 1 along left neck opening down to top left front corner, sc 2 into corner, sc 1 across left front edge. End with sl st.

Sew on buttons.

This project was knit with

(A) 6 balls of Lion Velvetspun, 100% polyester yarn, bulky weight, 3oz/85g = approx 54yd/49m per ball, color #580-100

Pompon Template 1

Pompon Template 2

Sole template

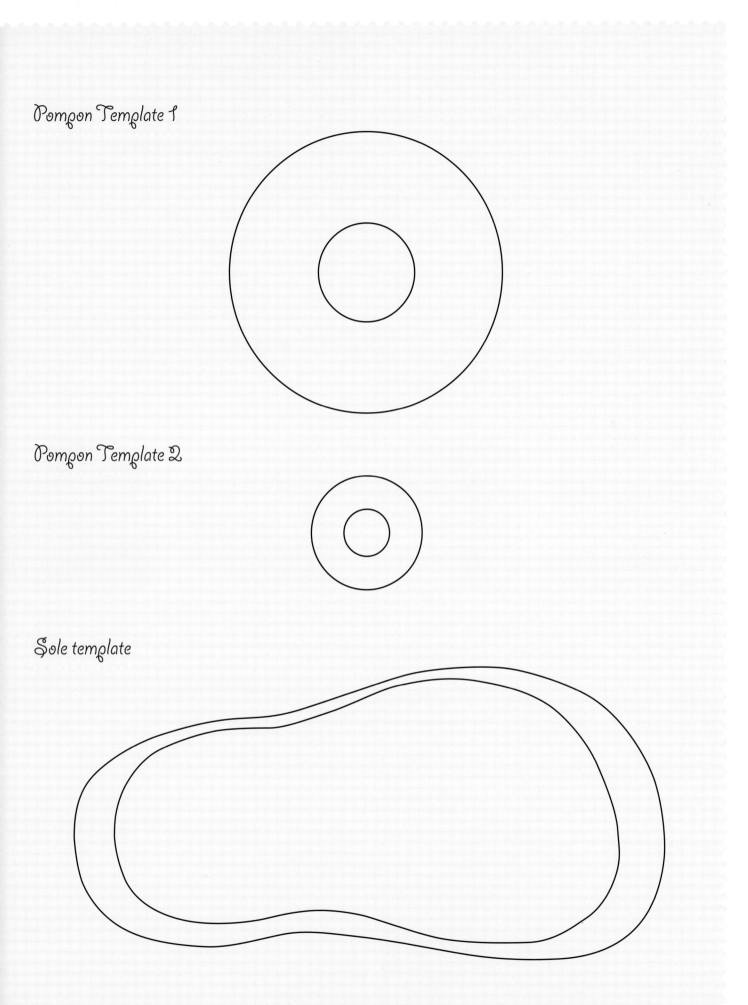